3 BIG QUESTIONS THAT SHAPE YOUR FUTURE

3 BIG QUESTIONS THAT SHAPE YOUR FUTURE

A 60-Day Exploration of Who You Were Made to Be

KARA POWELL, KRISTEL ACEVEDO, AND BRAD M. GRIFFIN

BakerBooks
a division of Baker Publishing Group
Grand Rapids, Michigan

Published by Baker Books
a division of Baker Publishing Group
PO Box 6287, Grand Rapids, MI 49516-6287
www.bakerbooks.com

Printed in the United States of America

Library of Congress Cataloging-in-Publication Data

Names: Powell, Kara Eckmann, 1970- author. | Acevedo, Kristel, author. | Griffin, Brad M., 1976- author.

Title: 3 big questions that shape your future : a 60-day exploration of who you were made to be / Kara E. Powell, Kristel Acevedo, and Brad M. Griffin.

Other titles: Three big questions that shape your future

Description: Grand Rapids, MI : Baker Books, a division of Baker Publishing Group, [2022] | Includes bibliographical references. | Audience: Ages 14–17 | Audience: Grades 10–12

Identifiers: LCCN 2022020835 | ISBN 9781540902443 (paperback) | ISBN 9781540902627 (casebound) | ISBN 9781493437795 (ebook)

Subjects: LCSH: Christian teenagers—Religious life. | Identity (Psychology)—Religious aspects—Christianity.

Classification: LCC BV4531.3 .P667 2022 | DDC 248.8/3—dc23/eng/20220808

LC record available at https://lccn.loc.gov/2022020835

Some names and details have been changed to protect the privacy of the individuals involved.

The authors are represented by WordServe Literary Group (www.wordserveliterary.com)

Baker Publishing Group publications use paper produced from sustainable forestry practices and post-consumer waste whenever possible.

22 23 24 25 26 27 28 7 6 5 4 3 2 1

Contents

INTRODUCTION

Asking the Right Questions

Life is all about questions.

And wow, there are *so many questions*.

Questions about the world.

Questions about the past.

Questions about the present.

Questions about the future—and more pointedly, about *your future*.

Maybe you feel the pressure to have everything figured out. Maybe you've thought the point of life is actually to find all the answers. Maybe you have adults around you who make it seem like that's *your* job, which feels stressful.

We want to let you in on something up front: this is not that kind of book.

Embracing the Questions

We may not know you personally, but we've spent a lot of time with young people like you. We are youth leaders who serve in churches and researchers who listen to teenagers talk about life and faith. We hear a lot of questions, and we ask a lot of questions.

This book is about embracing the questions.

Because the answers aren't the whole point. Questions take us on a journey, and the act of exploring, wondering, seeking, even wrestling our way toward answers changes us—sometimes as much as the answers themselves.

Over the course of this book, we'll each share a few of our own stories of wrestling with big questions. Since there are three of us, we'll clarify whose story is whose by adding our names in parentheses the first time we say "I" in a post. One thing you should know though: asking a lot of questions is what landed each of us where we are today.

Brad used to get in trouble for asking too many questions in school. He couldn't help asking questions that started with "But what about . . . ?" Yes, he drove his teachers crazy.

Kristel is naturally curious and would always ask her parents "Why . . . ?" She wanted to know how and why the world functioned as it did and what it all meant. She's still looking for answers.

And Kara especially used to love asking questions in church. All the better if she could stump her youth pastor and small group leader.

So if you're a question asker already, we're here to say *you're not alone*. If, on the other hand, you tend to shy away from questions, or if asking questions stresses you out, you're also not alone. We've written this as a guide you can use wherever you are in your journey.

Here's more good news: questions aren't new to God. By one count of the four Gospels, Jesus was asked 183 questions.[1]

That's remarkable, but what's even more remarkable is that Jesus himself asked 307 questions. If he was comfortable with questions *then*, he's comfortable with questions *now*.

So maybe we shouldn't worry whether God can handle our questions.

Easier said than done, right?

All the same, we know what it's like to not feel safe enough to ask what we really want—or to not have the tools and guides we need to explore our questions and even wrestle down some answers.

The 3 Big Questions underneath the Rest

Based on our research with over two thousand teenagers, we've learned a lot about your generation. We heard from young people like you that among the dozens of questions tumbling through any teenager's mind at any time, the following often float to the top.

Who am I? The question of *identity*.
Where do I fit? The question of *belonging*.
What difference can I make? The question of *purpose*.

These aren't questions just for young people; they're questions for everyone. Adults still wonder about these things too. The three of us sure do! It's just that the period of life you're in right now is one that tends to push the big questions to the surface more often.

We've put this book together as a guide for you to explore these questions for yourself. You won't be alone. We'll be here, and we'll tell the stories of other teenagers and some stories from the Bible and stories from historical figures along the way. Whenever we directly quote a young person from our research, we use a pseudonym we've given them to protect their privacy. So anyone we reference by just a first name (like Lilly, Daniel, or Armando) is a real teenager like you who participated in up to six hours of interviews over the course of three visits.

While we based our work on research, we haven't weighed this book down with lots of citations. All the background and notes can be found in *3 Big Questions That Change Every Teenager*, which was written for adults but might be interesting to you if you're into research (like us).

How to Use This Book

Notice we didn't say "How to *read* this book." It is, of course, a book, and we do want you to read it. But we hope it is more like a guide—something useful, offering directions and insights along your journey.

Each post includes a story or some thoughts that introduce the idea, followed by these sections:

- *Reading God's Word*
  Sometimes the Bible passage will be the main focus of the day; other times it will offer a way to reflect on the ideas we've shared. The verses are written out for you here, but we encourage you to look them up in your own Bible or your favorite Bible app—that way you can mark them for yourself,

see where the passage fits into a chapter and book, and read more if you're curious. Sometimes we'll share only part of a passage, so having your Bible open alongside the book will help you see what else is there.[2]

- *Reflect and Respond*

  We've written a few prompts and journaling questions to get you thinking. You can either write your reflections here in the book or use a separate journal for more writing, drawing, or whatever helps you process.

  There's also a starter prayer you can pray. Sometimes it's helpful to have words to use, but if that's not your style, you can just pray your own prayer!
- *Something to Try*

  Each post offers something you can do to turn your questions into action. All of the suggestions may not work for you, but we encourage you to try as many as you can. You might find a few practices you want to repeat or make a regular part of your rhythms.
- *The Takeaway*

  One last thought for the road—short and sweet.

There are sixty posts in all, divided between the big questions of identity, belonging, and purpose. Here are a few ideas for how you might tackle the content:

- Read one entry every day or a few days a week or whatever pace works for you. If you already have a regular pattern of reading Scripture or using a devotional guide, this is meant to be used in that way.
- Whatever your pace of reading these posts, you can either read them straight through, or start with the section you're most interested in exploring, then circle back to the others.
- Read with a group. Big questions love company! Maybe you're already part of a small group and you can work through this together. Or maybe you want to ask a few

friends to join you and form your own group. If you go this route, we recommend setting a regular day and time to meet and deciding together which posts you'll read ahead of each session.

- Use it with a mentor or family member. Sometimes it's helpful to get outside perspective on our big questions. Maybe an adult you trust could be a sounding board while you process what comes up while you read, write, and try new things throughout this guide.
- Mark it up! Underline words and phrases that stand out to you. Write notes, questions, or comments in the margins. Fold down the corners of pages you want to circle back to or find again quickly.

However you choose to use this book, we want it to be shame-free. We didn't list dates or days of the week or anything like that on the posts because we wanted you to have a guide that can flex with what fits you best.

If some of the language we use is new to you, or if Christianity altogether is new to you or something you're checking out, we hope this guide can be a sort of "way in," a start down a new road.

As you go, you might find even more questions bubbling up in you. That's a good thing. Remember that finding answers isn't necessarily the point. Both life and faith are, at their core, kind of a mystery.

If questions lead you to more questions, that's no sign of *failure*. It's a sign of *growth*.

So let's get started right now. What do you wonder about? What questions bug you about your life now or what your life will be like someday? What do you wonder about your future? Go ahead and write down a few of your own big questions. Don't hold back!

> *Who am I?*

Where do I fit?

What difference can I make?

My other questions . . .

PART 1

WHO AM I?

The Big Question of
IDENTITY

> Every day, I don't ever forget who I am. And I don't ever let anyone tell me who I am.
>
> Jason

Wow, Jason is more confident than I (Kara) was at his age.

As a teenager, I often let myself be defined by who I was around. I was "smart Kara" at school, "Christian Kara" at church, "fun Kara" around my friends, and "work-hard Kara" on my swim team.

Most teenagers we interviewed are more like me than Jason.

Most teenagers also struggle with feeling inadequate. With feeling like they don't measure up.

As a teenager, I never felt like I was enough. Thirty years later, I still struggle with knowing that who I am is sufficient.

That's why the message of this section on identity is that you and I are ENOUGH because of Jesus.

We don't have to try so hard to win everyone's approval or become their preferred version of us. God says we are ENOUGH because we are created in God's image as beloved children. We are whole regardless of others' expectations and disappointments.

Every post in part 1 helps you live with more confidence that Jesus makes you more than ENOUGH. That's one of my daily prayers for myself, and I want it to be your daily reality.

With so many voices telling us who we are, it's important that we remember our identity is ultimately found in Christ. And Jesus says we are *ENOUGH*.

POST 1

Who People Expect You to Be vs. Who God Expects You to Be

> "I just really, really, really cared about what other people thought about me. And I really wanted to have the right friends and do the right things." She pointed her finger at a handful of imaginary people: "I was whatever I wanted to be for you, and for you, and for you. I didn't have any stability. I kept looking for satisfaction, but none of it was working."
>
> Rebekah

I (Brad) love theater. In middle school, acting saved me from isolation and even depression.

A lot of that love came from my drama teacher, Mrs. Dwyer. Starting in sixth grade, she saw something in me that others didn't: the potential to take my over-the-top personality and extra-loud voice and channel both toward public speaking and performance. At her invitation, I joined the speech and drama team and never looked back. (It's possible she regretted this invitation; at times, I was a bit much.)

Acting opened up an entire world of possibilities for me—and one of the most exciting parts was getting to pretend I was someone else for a while.

When Pretending Gets Complicated

Acting is great when it's on an actual stage for fun. But not when it's your real life.

Maybe you find that each day feels like a live performance in front of a packed audience. On the far right of the theater sits your family. The center of the audience is full of friends from school, work, sports, and your neighborhood.

Just to the left are members of your church. Next to church members sit rows of teachers, coaches, and mentors.

In the front row are the people who follow you on social media, while perched in the balcony sit influencers telling you how to measure your beauty and achievement.

Your task: to try to please every audience member. At every moment. You can't just be yourself; you have to be your *best self*—whatever that means.

It's exhausting.

More than that, it's *impossible*. No one can do it.

The best of us can please only one audience at a time. But as we bounce from group to group, we're often swapping scripts. So we end up defining ourselves this way: *I am what others want or need me to be. I constantly feel pressure to live up to everyone else's expectations.*

All our lives, our identities are shaped by others. But you're in a stage of life when others' influence is massive. The thing is, while you may feel like you have to meet everyone's expectations all the time, God doesn't see you that way.

God doesn't expect you to be perfect or to meet a long list of requirements. God created you the way you are and is joyfully watching your personality, gifts, and unique quirks unfold. God's expectation is that you will be *you*—the person God created, not the person everyone else expects or pressures you to be.

We see this in the story of Jesus' own baptism. When he was dipped under the water and raised up again, the voice of God spoke a blessing over him: "You are my Son, whom I love; with you I am well pleased" (Mark 1:11 NIV). This was before Jesus had done anything in his ministry to prove he was good enough for a blessing—no followers, no miracles, no teaching. He was loved, and his Father was pleased with him without any performance.

When I think back to the real power of Mrs. Dwyer's influence on my life, it reached far beyond a skill set. In a season when I was experiencing intense social rejection, she never once made me feel left out, weird, or alone.

She didn't just see something *in* me—she saw *me*. That gift profoundly shaped who I am today. Because who I am is enough.

READING GOD'S WORD

> At that time Jesus came from Nazareth in Galilee and was baptized by John in the Jordan. Just as Jesus was coming up out of the water, he saw heaven being torn open and the Spirit descending on him like a dove. And a voice came from heaven: "You are my Son, whom I love; with you I am well pleased." (Mark 1:9–11 NIV)

REFLECT AND RESPOND

Journaling Questions

> How often do you feel like your identity is caught up in others' expectations? How does that make you feel about yourself?

> List some of the unique qualities God's given you. How would you describe who you really are beyond the expectations or opinions of others? It's okay if you're not sure or if you write characteristics that seem opposite one another; that's part of

discovering who you are! Just write a snapshot of who you are today.

What does it mean to you to read that God is "well pleased" with you? How might knowing that impact the way you see yourself?

Pray This Prayer

God who created me and knows me, thank you for loving me for who I am. I spend a lot of energy trying to be what other people want me to be. Help me to live each day knowing that I am who you made me to be, and let that be enough. In Jesus' name, amen.

SOMETHING TO TRY

Flip the script. Pick an audience in your life with whom you're working too hard to act according to a script that doesn't feel authentically you. Where are you performing for the expectations of others? Imagine what it would look like to flip that script in some way—maybe it's saying no when you typically say yes, giving an unpopular opinion, or deciding not to post a perfectly curated picture or video. Pay attention to what it feels like to choose to be yourself.

THE TAKEAWAY

Acting is great when you're on a stage, but God didn't put you on a permanent stage. Be your offstage self today.

POST 2

How Does God View You?

I (Kristel) started actively following Jesus when I was a teenager. It was a confusing time as I ventured out to understand who I was and what role my new faith played in my journey of self-discovery.

The message I often received in churches and youth groups was that I was fundamentally flawed—sinful. I often wondered if God looked at me with disgust. Each time I stumbled, I gave myself a hard time and pictured God being irritated with me. How could God even stand the sight of me? I needed to do better and earn God's love.

Grace may have been good enough to save me, but it wasn't enough to keep me saved. God clearly expected me to pull myself up by my bootstraps, quit slacking off, and get myself together. Or so I thought.

Look Again

While we are all born with sin, it's not obligation that causes God to save us; it's love. It took me a long time, but one day I realized that God looks at me the way I look at my own children now—with awe and affection.

John 3:16 is the first verse I ever memorized: "God so loved the world that he gave his only Son, so that everyone who believes in him won't perish but will have eternal life." Did you catch it? God *so loved*. That's the reason God sent Jesus to this earth. Rather than looking down on us and our sin with anger or frustration, God looks at us with love and compassion. Verse 17 further clarifies that God didn't send Jesus to judge or condemn us but to save us. God wanted better for us and would do whatever it took to rescue us from our mess.

At my church, we say that we love God completely, love ourselves correctly, and love our neighbors compassionately. When I meet with my small group of high school girls, I often find myself reminding them about the part that says "love ourselves correctly." They feel so much pressure to look a certain way or get good grades or be perfect. Sometimes without thinking they will say something like "Ugh, I look terrible!" or "I'm so dumb" or "Sorry, I'm not wearing any makeup today!" When I hear comments like that, I take the opportunity to gently remind them that loving yourself correctly means talking to yourself kindly and remembering that you can show up just as you are without apology.

I love having conversations with them and helping them see that we are not meant to hate ourselves or put ourselves down. We look together at where God declares faithful love for us in Scripture. God calls us good and desires to be with us.

Even when we mess up, God's love for us doesn't change. When we stumble and fall, God doesn't scoff at us and wait for us to stand and dust ourselves off. Instead, God wraps loving arms around us and holds us. God helps us to our feet and directs us forward in a new way. That's what grace is.

If you ever question how God sees you, remember this: you are God's creation, God's child. God gave everything to be with you—right now and forever. God loves you with an everlasting, unending love.

READING GOD'S WORD

God so loved the world that he gave his only Son, so that everyone who believes in him won't perish but will have eternal life. God didn't send

> his Son into the world to judge the world, but that the world might be saved through him. (John 3:16–17)

> See what kind of love the Father has given to us in that we should be called God's children, and that is what we are! Because the world didn't recognize him, it doesn't recognize us.
>
> Dear friends, now we are God's children, and it hasn't yet appeared what we will be. We know that when he appears we will be like him because we'll see him as he is. And all who have this hope in him purify themselves even as he is pure. (1 John 3:1–3)

REFLECT AND RESPOND

Journaling Questions

In the past, what have you been taught about the way God views you? How is that similar to or different from what you read today?

How do you know God loves you? What might make you question that love? What might help you be more confident in it?

How might knowing you are loved by God help you love yourself?

Pray This Prayer

God, loving myself correctly can seem impossible at times. When I don't love myself, help me to remember that you love me with an infinite and unconditional love. Help me to see myself the way you see me. In Jesus' name, amen.

SOMETHING TO TRY

Today, pay close attention to the way you speak to yourself. Each time you catch your negative self-talk, stop and speak truth instead. If you're not sure the best truth to focus on at the moment, remind yourself that you are loved by God.

THE TAKEAWAY

No matter how you look at yourself, God looks at you with unending love.

POST 3

What to Do When Being Labeled Holds You Back

I (Kara) was known as the "smart" kid in the family. Since kindergarten, studying and getting good grades have both been pretty natural for me.

My brother was the funny one—always cracking jokes and making our family laugh.

My stepsister was the athlete. She excelled at any sport she tried (well, except basketball, but that was because she didn't know the rules so she kept fouling out).

My stepbrother was the creative and curious one. From dismantling sprinklers across our block (which got him into trouble) to diving into computers when they first became popular (which got him into his programming career), he's perpetually eager to figure out how stuff works.

We didn't discuss these labels aloud, but they still came to define us—first in our family, but also in our friend groups.

How about you? In your family or in your friend group, which label fits you? Are you the smart, funny, athletic, or creative one—like me and my siblings?

Or maybe you're the artistic one.

Or the romantic one.

Or the wild one.

Or the spiritual one.

Or the outgoing or introverted one.

Those sorts of labels—that others say aloud or we think ourselves—are hard to avoid. While labels are not entirely bad, they tend to limit us at times.

Labels Limit Us

Labels limit us when we stay stuck in certain understandings of who we are and don't allow ourselves to change. If we think that we're only creative and not also potentially introverted or funny, we can shortchange ourselves and miss out on parts of who God has made us to be.

Labels limit us when we feel like we have to be what others expect—even if it's not who we are or what we feel at that moment. Sometimes it's not our view of ourselves that limits us but others' views. If we feel like we always have to be the "happy one" at home to cheer up Grandpa, or the "good youth group kid" at church so our youth pastor likes us, we miss out on the full spectrum of emotions God's given us. We end up denying some of our feelings, which can make us feel fake.

Labels limit us when we forget that more than anything else, we are defined as people who are made in God's image and loved by God. God has made each of us as unique individuals, and our unique qualities often come to define us. No one can change the fundamental truths of who God made us to be. They define us more than even our standout athletic, academic, artistic, or social skills.

Even Jesus was dogged by labels. Being from Nazareth was an insult at the time, but Jesus turned the insult around. In John 1, he gives Nathanael a compliment, catching him off guard and sharing a vision that transcended any simple label.

When we choose to follow Jesus, *this* identity surrounds all others and becomes part of all we are.

READING GOD'S WORD

The next day Jesus wanted to go into Galilee, and he found Philip. Jesus said to him, "Follow me." Philip was from Bethsaida, the hometown of Andrew and Peter.

Philip found Nathanael and said to him, "We have found the one Moses wrote about in the Law and the Prophets: Jesus, Joseph's son, from Nazareth."

Nathanael responded, "Can anything from Nazareth be good?"

Philip said, "Come and see."

Jesus saw Nathanael coming toward him and said about him, "Here is a genuine Israelite in whom there is no deceit."

Nathanael asked him, "How do you know me?" (John 1:43–48)

REFLECT AND RESPOND

Journaling Questions

What are the labels you would use to describe yourself? What are the labels others would use to describe you?

Which of these labels do you love? Which would you change if you could?

How do these qualities compare with your identity as a Jesus follower?

Pray This Prayer

God, thank you for the skills and personality you have given me. I'm sorry for the way I let other labels define me. I want to be more defined by my relationship with you than by anything else. Please help me to view myself first as a follower of yours—above anything else. In Jesus' name, amen.

SOMETHING TO TRY

On your phone or on a piece of paper, draw a fairly large circle in the center. Label that circle "Jesus follower." Then draw a handful of other surrounding circles and write a label next to each of them—such as daughter, athlete, close friend. The bigger the circle, the more important the label is to you. If being a Jesus follower isn't yet your biggest circle, that's okay. Be honest with where you are now and come back to this exercise as you grow.

If there are other aspects of yourself that you'd like to explore further (such as being more of an introvert or sad or angry), then add those circles in a different color or label them with a different font. Keep this diagram somewhere you can pull it out from time to time as a reminder of the value in having Jesus define you more than anything else. Let it encourage you to keep exploring more aspects of who God has made you.

THE TAKEAWAY

The more you follow Jesus, the more your relationship with Jesus defines you.

POST 4

What It Means to Be Fearfully and Wonderfully Made

When you look in the mirror or scroll through the photos on your phone, what do you see?

When you think about your personality, what do you feel?

Being a teenager can often feel awkward and uncomfortable. During these years, we begin to discover who we are, what we like, what we don't like, and who we want to be as we enter adulthood.

It may not surprise you that a lot of teenagers don't really like the way they were made. They feel that something must be missing—that they're lacking in some way. They feel confused about who they really are and may even try to change themselves to fit a certain image. Or maybe who they are is a mystery to them. One teenager told us, "I didn't really know who I was. And I didn't really care either. And I was like, 'Wait, why isn't this working out?'"

Here's the thing: just because you don't feel like you were made very well doesn't make it true. Your feelings don't determine truth. God does.

What Does God Say about Me?

Psalm 139 is a beautiful reminder of how God sees us. Think of it as a window into God's thoughts and feelings for you.

Psalm 139 is really a Hebrew poem that tells us God is all-present, all-knowing, and all-powerful. In other words, God is everywhere and can do anything, and yet, God still looks at each one of us individually as a unique creation. God looks at you with care and love—and desires to have a relationship with you. Take a moment to think about that. The God of the universe who can do anything and be anywhere and knows everything also knows you and wants to be with you.

Psalm 139 takes us on a journey. First, we are introduced to the remarkable fact that God knows us and is paying attention to the intimate details of our lives—when we stand up and when we lie down. God is familiar with all our ways. Every word we speak has already been known. In verse 7, the psalmist describes how God is ever present. There is never a moment in which we are alone. God is always with us.

In verses 13–18, we see God's creative intentionality with us, forming us in our mother's womb. God created every detail with purpose.

Verse 14 says, "I praise you because I am fearfully and wonderfully made; your works are wonderful, I know that full well" (NIV). Perhaps you've heard this before. *Fearfully and wonderfully*. What does that even mean?

The original Hebrew word for *fearfully* means "with great reverence, heartfelt interest, and with respect." That's how God made you—with great admiration and awe. God is deeply interested in you and appreciates who you are.

Toward the end of the psalm, we are assured that God is a God of justice who comes through for creation. And finally, the psalmist worships God. Now that the psalmist knows who God is and what God has done, they know who they are and how to respond: with awe and wonder.

God made you with intentionality and purpose. God marvels at you because you are God's own creation. And God thinks you're pretty wonderful.

Sometimes reading the same verse in multiple translations helps us see that verse from different perspectives and adds to our understanding. As you read through the various translations of verse 14 in the following section, how does your understanding of the truth found in it grow?

READING GOD'S WORD

I praise you because of the wonderful way you created me. Everything you do is marvelous! Of this I have no doubt. (CEV)

I give thanks to you that I was marvelously set apart.
Your works are wonderful—I know that very well. (CEB)

Thank you for making me so wonderfully complex! Your workmanship is marvelous—how well I know it. (NLT)

REFLECT AND RESPOND

Journaling Questions

How do you view yourself? How does it differ from the way God views you? How is it similar?

What did you learn from Psalm 139 that you didn't know before?

What does being "fearfully and wonderfully made" mean to you?

Pray This Prayer

God, I praise you because I am fearfully and wonderfully made. Whenever I start to forget this truth, remind me that I am yours and you made me with intention and purpose. In Jesus' name, amen.

SOMETHING TO TRY

Write your own psalm to God, giving praise for the unique ways you were created. Be as detailed as possible. It doesn't have to be long or poetic; what's most important is that it captures what you're feeling and thinking about yourself and the God who made you.

THE TAKEAWAY

God is wonderful—and made you wonderful.

POST 5

God's Intentional Design for Your Ethnicity

Kevin is a self-described "Blasian" twelfth grader. He embraces both his Black and his Asian background, and so he understands the tensions that come with race and ethnicity. He feels the pressure to conform to certain aspects of his ethnic groups. As a result, he pushes against others' stereotypes and expectations about his cultural background. It can be tricky to navigate.

Racial tensions are as old as time. When we look at the history of racial relations in the US, we see centuries of oppression, prejudice, violence, and death. In Old Testament stories, we read that tensions between the Israelites and other people groups turned into wars. In Jesus' day, the Romans brutally oppressed the Jews—and the Samaritans were mortal enemies of the Jewish people, despite their shared history. While they may not have understood *race* the same way we do, ethnic and cultural differences fueled all this hatred.

What's the Point?

The tensions Kevin shared are echoed in a scene from the movie *Selena* about the life and career of Mexican American musical artist Selena. While her family was Mexican by ancestry, they were living in the US and had to try to navigate both cultures. In the scene, Selena, her brother, and her dad are having a conversation about the pressures of being Mexican American. The dad talks about the racism he experienced growing up and how they must speak both Spanish *and* English perfectly. They have to be Mexican enough for the Mexicans and American enough for the Americans. "It's exhausting!" he laments.[1]

What do we make of all the strife people experience because of their ethnic identity? Should we all be "color-blind" in an attempt not to see these ethnic identities? Will that ease the tensions and lead to harmony?

Our answer to those last two questions is a resounding no. That's because God, as an intentional Creator, has a purpose for all our racial, ethnic, and cultural identities.

In Genesis 1:27, we read about the *imago Dei*, the image of God. God creates humanity in God's own divine image. We all carry the image of God within us, and yet, we are each vastly different. How can that be?

To be made in God's image means that we each have intrinsic value. We are all *equally* valued. The fact that we all are so different, though, tells us we also have *unique* value.

Here's one way to think about this: since we each reflect God's image and we are all diverse, we each reflect a different aspect of God's image. It's when we all come together that we get a fuller picture of who God is. Your ethnic identity is a part of that. Your language, accent, food, traditions, skin color—they all matter, and they all show us who God is in some way.

If you've ever felt shame or confusion over your ethnic identity, remember that when God created you, God wanted the world to see a unique aspect of God's image in you. No matter what anyone says or thinks, you can be certain that your ethnic identity is important and an intentional part of God's design.

READING GOD'S WORD

God created humanity in God's own image, in the divine image God created them, male and female God created them. (Genesis 1:27)

After this I looked, and there was a great crowd that no one could number. They were from every nation, tribe, people, and language. They were standing before the throne and before the Lamb. They wore white robes and held palm branches in their hands. (Revelation 7:9)

REFLECT AND RESPOND

Journaling Questions

What is your ethnic and cultural identity? In what ways has that identity shaped you?

What gifts do you bring to the world because of your cultural heritage?

How might knowing you're made in God's image help you navigate racial tension or stereotypes?

Pray This Prayer

Thank you, God, for your unique creativity in making me. My race, ethnicity, and culture are not coincidences. Instead, they reflect a unique aspect of your image. Help me to see my unique identity as beautiful and needed. In Jesus' name, amen.

SOMETHING TO TRY

Take some time to research your ethnic and cultural identity. Is there someone in your family who can provide answers? Perhaps a parent or grandparent can tell you more about your family history. If this isn't an option, you can research about your ethnic and cultural identity online. What's something new you can learn about this part of your identity? Think about someone with whom you can share what you're learning.

THE TAKEAWAY

God created you with a unique background so you can uniquely reflect God's image to the world. Your ethnicity and culture are part of God's design for who you are.

POST 6

How Who You Are Is Shaped by Where You Live

Where do you live?

When you think about that question, your mind probably goes to geography: your country, state, community, neighborhood; your house or apartment. You might think less about a different kind of geography: your *social location.*

Social location means the way you're shaped by not only your physical surroundings but also your gender, race, ethnicity, social class, age, ability, religion, and sexual orientation. The way you operate in life is deeply impacted by your social location. While you can educate yourself and become aware of this impact, you can never fully distance yourself from it.

That's not a bad thing. It's simply something to be aware of.

Building Bridges

In the varied ethnic world we live in today, you may have the opportunity to cross boundaries and build cultural bridges. Maybe you can relate to Claudia, a seventeen-year-old Latina who loves traditional Mexican dishes but also enjoys Korean drinks and treats. She intentionally introduces her Latino friends to Korean cuisine and invites her Korean friends to enjoy Mexican food in her home and neighborhood.

While this cultural exchange can at times create tension for Claudia, she also enjoys watching both sets of friends try new foods. Claudia summarized: "Although I get to try some of their culture, I also get to share some of mine, and they actually love it. It's so fun."

Sometimes when we encounter someone from a different social location, we can feel uncomfortable or even threatened. Instead of allowing those fears to overtake us, we can remind ourselves of what we can learn and how fun—and meaningful—it can be to experience a different culture.

You may find that you are changed when you go out of your way to listen to, love, and learn from people who are from different social locations. You can also help others learn and grow when you share your perspective. You have a unique, valid, and significant point of view.

Never forget that God created you in your distinct social location for a reason. God wants you to share—and God also wants you to listen.

In the book of Acts, the apostle Paul encounters the people of Athens. His social location and that of the Athenians were vastly different. He could have condemned their idol worship and way of life; instead, he observed their culture and traditions and tapped into these to share the gospel with them. He was even able to use their own poetry to illustrate the beauty of God's divine nature.

The more awareness we have of our social location, the more opportunities we will have to build bridges. It won't always be easy; in fact, it's often really hard! Sometimes people don't want to work on your part of the bridge. That's okay. We can respect where people are in their journeys while keeping the door open.

READING GOD'S WORD

Paul stood up in the middle of the council on Mars Hill and said, "People of Athens, I see that you are very religious in every way. As I was walking through town and carefully observing your objects of worship, I even found an altar with this inscription: 'To an unknown God.' What you worship as unknown, I now proclaim to you. God, who made the world and everything in it, is Lord of heaven and earth. He doesn't live in temples made with human hands. Nor is God served by human hands, as though he needed something, since he is the one who gives life, breath, and everything else. From one person God created every human nation to live on the whole earth, having determined their appointed times and the boundaries of their lands. God made the nations so they would seek him, perhaps even reach out to him and find him. In fact, God isn't far away from any of us. In God we live, move, and exist. As some of your own poets said, 'We are his offspring.'" (Acts 17:22–28)

REFLECT AND RESPOND

Journaling Questions

Take an audit of your social location. What is your gender, race, ethnicity, social class, age, ability, religion, sexual orientation, and geography?

How does your social location impact your view of the world? How does it impact the way others see you?

How and when can you engage someone of a different social location?

Pray This Prayer

God, you have made me in a unique way with a unique perspective. Help me to understand how it all impacts my point of view, and help me to be open to learning from those who have a different social location. In Jesus' name, amen.

SOMETHING TO TRY

Take a cue from Claudia and build a bridge from one culture to another. For example, invite two friends from different backgrounds and try foods from each person's culture. Learn about the origin of each dish so you can appreciate both the differences and the similarities.

THE TAKEAWAY

Your social location is unique and valuable—and so are the social locations of others.

POST 7

When You Feel Like a Misfit

> I think a lot about what other people think of me . . . whether or not somebody likes me. Whether they thought what I said was weird or stuff like that. I envy the people who are like "I don't really care." I wish that was me, but it's not.
>
> Sue

In a story in John 4, it was the hottest part of the day—a time of day when most people avoided the water well. So what was *she* doing there?

Fetching water was seen as a community activity. The women of the village would gather in the cool of the morning and talk as they drew water for the day. The fact that this Samaritan woman was at the well alone at noon already tells us she's an outsider, a misfit.

Her conversation with Jesus tells us more. She's had many husbands and has been labeled as undesirable and unwelcome. We don't know the full story of how she wound up in this position, but we do know in that time only men could divorce their wives and not the other way around. If the Samaritan woman had been married and divorced several times, it's likely because her husbands abandoned her.

Maybe she was alone at the well because she wanted to avoid having to mingle with the other women. She likely felt unworthy to even be in their presence. Or just tired of being made to feel that way. (You can read the entire story in John 4:4–42.)

Lunchtime Alone

Picture a cafeteria with students gathered around tables, talking excitedly about weekend plans as they eat lunch. Each table is filled with friends laughing and sharing stories.

Then there's that one table where a girl sits alone, fidgeting with her fries. She doesn't dress the same as everyone else and doesn't have many friends. In fact, rumors have been circulating about her. Who she is, where she came from, what she did that one night with you-know-who. She feels alone and unworthy. She doesn't dare raise her eyes to look at anyone for fear that too much attention will come her way. It's better to lie low so the whispers don't start up again.

That girl sits alone, but Jesus didn't leave the Samaritan woman alone. In fact, he went out of his way to meet her at the well. He spoke to her in a time when Jews and Samaritans hated one another, and a rabbi wouldn't be caught dead speaking to a Samaritan woman of her reputation. He threw the social rules out the window and shared with her something he had not told anyone—something special and profound.

Jesus tells her that he is the "I Am" (v. 26). The Messiah. The Christ. The Savior. God in flesh. He uses the Old Testament name for God, "I Am," to confirm to this woman that he is, in fact, the one they have all been waiting for. It's weird; instead of going to the most respected person in town, he chooses a woman who has been discarded by her community—a misfit.

That's one of the beautiful things about Jesus.

He draws near to those who feel alone, rejected, and on the outs. He's not scared of the rumors or the oddities. He welcomes the outcast, gives them a place of honor, and offers them "living water"—because we all belong to him. Our ultimate identity is not rejected, abandoned, victim, unworthy, outcast, misfit. No, our ultimate identity is welcomed, worthy, child of God.

READING GOD'S WORD

The Samaritan woman asked, "Why do you, a Jewish man, ask for something to drink from me, a Samaritan woman?" (Jews and Samaritans didn't associate with each other.)

Jesus responded, "If you recognized God's gift and who is saying to you, 'Give me some water to drink,' you would be asking him and he would give you living water."

The woman said to him, "Sir, you don't have a bucket and the well is deep. Where would you get this living water? You aren't greater than our father Jacob, are you? He gave this well to us, and he drank from it himself, as did his sons and his livestock."

Jesus answered, "Everyone who drinks this water will be thirsty again, but whoever drinks from the water that I will give will never be thirsty again. The water that I give will become in those who drink it a spring of water that bubbles up into eternal life." (John 4:9–14)

REFLECT AND RESPOND

Journaling Questions

> When have you felt like an outcast or a misfit? Did anyone reach out to you to bring you in?

> What does Jesus say to the misfits? How does knowing Jesus welcomes everyone in make you feel?

> Is there someone around you who might feel like a misfit? How can you show them Jesus' kind of love?

Pray This Prayer

God, there are times when I feel like a misfit. I wonder where I fit and why I'm not accepted. But the truth is I'm not rejected by you. You love me, accept me, welcome me, and give me a place of honor. When doubt creeps in, remind me of your truth. In Jesus' name, amen.

SOMETHING TO TRY

Is there a community in your city in which the people are treated like outcasts? This could be the unhoused, refugees, or any other group forgotten or pushed to the margins by society. Research how you can serve among this community and remind its members that they are loved and accepted.

THE TAKEAWAY

Misfits are welcomed by Jesus. Our ultimate identity is in a status given to us not by the world but by God.

POST 8

When You Struggle with Perfectionism

Have you ever been called a perfectionist? Perfectionism is something that impacts people from all walks of life. The pressure to perform perfectly can add stress in our lives and even cause us to hide who we really are for fear that it's not "good enough."

Carrie is a youth pastor in a high-pressure, affluent Minneapolis suburb who was wrestling with how her students seemed to be stuck in relationally shallow waters. She knew there was great pain hidden under the surface, but any time struggle or pain started to be expressed, the default was to stuff it down or ignore it. Carrie knew something had to change, and over time God helped her create an environment in which students felt safe enough to be vulnerable.

Janelle's parents see her as confident and smart. She's self-assured, but others' opinions also really matter to her. This year she started serving as a leader in her school's Black Student Union. She feels continual pressure—internally and externally—to perform academically: "I feel like I have to do everything so perfect." Janelle constantly lives in the messy middle of the different ways in which she identifies: young, Black, female, smart, confident, anxious.

Lilly plummets emotionally when she makes a mistake. Mistakes "bum me out for like the whole day. I know it is human to make mistakes. But it just makes me feel really bad."

Perfectly Imperfect

How do you feel when you make mistakes? When the world is about to see that you're not perfect? Do you go into panic mode? Do you feel bad about yourself?

The apostle Paul was seen as basically perfect by the standards of his community. In Philippians 3, he lists his credentials: he was a Jewish man with an impeccable record, an expert at all things God-related. While he used to be really proud of all this, he came to see that his list was nothing to boast about. He would always fall short of perfection, but in Christ he had been given a goodness that was not from his own doing but from the faithfulness of Jesus. This changed everything for Paul.

When we recognize we are accepted because of Christ and what he has done and not because of anything we do, it changes our perspective. The weight of perfectionism is lifted off our shoulders, and we can taste freedom.

Let yourself off the hook. You don't have to be perfect; Jesus already is.

READING GOD'S WORD

But even beyond that, I consider everything a loss in comparison with the superior value of knowing Christ Jesus my Lord. I have lost everything for him, but what I lost I think of as sewer trash, so that I might gain Christ and be found in him. In Christ I have a righteousness that is not my own and that does not come from the Law but rather from the faithfulness of Christ. It is the righteousness of God that is based on faith. The righteousness that I have comes from knowing Christ, the power of his resurrection, and the participation in his sufferings. It includes being conformed to his death so that I may perhaps reach the goal of the resurrection of the dead. (Philippians 3:8–11)

REFLECT AND RESPOND

Journaling Questions

> Do you struggle with perfectionism? This can show up in many ways—from academically to physically to maintaining a certain image. How does perfectionism show up in you?

> How can you let yourself off the hook when it comes to perfectionism? How does Jesus let us all off the hook of perfectionism?

Pray This Prayer

God, when I struggle to be perfect, remind me that you are the perfect one. When I am tempted to hide my imperfections, remind me that I am free to live an authentic and vulnerable life. When I try to maintain an impossible standard, remind me that I don't have to perform to be loved and accepted. In Jesus' name, amen.

SOMETHING TO TRY

Talk with a trusted adult about their own struggles with perfectionism. You may be surprised to see that many others can relate to this struggle. Ask them how they have overcome the need to be perfect in their own life and look for encouragement to do the same in your life. Discuss Philippians 3 and get their perspective on how we don't have to feel the pressure to perform.

THE TAKEAWAY

Get free of the perfection trap and run toward being real.

POST 9

When You Feel Underestimated

Imagine being the youngest boy in a family full of boys. Competition and comparison are common as each son tries to prove he is the best and strongest and fastest.

If you've heard the story of David and Goliath, then you probably know David was underestimated. David was young and small. When he visited his older brothers on the battlefield and questioned why none of the soldiers would go up against Goliath, the larger-than-life Philistine warrior, people wondered what his aim was. "You can't fight this Philistine. You're just a youth, and he's been a warrior since he was young."

Just a youth. Has anyone made a similar comment to you?

"You're *just* a teenager."

"You're *just* a girl."

"You're *just* an academic kid."

"You're *just* an athlete."

If so, you're in good company. David, too, was underestimated, but he proved them all wrong when he defeated Goliath with a slingshot (and, of course, the power of the Lord).

David's Backstory

When we look back at David's story, we see that he was underestimated long before he dared to face Goliath. In 1 Samuel 16:4–13, the prophet Samuel is on the lookout for a new king. The Lord directs him to Bethlehem, where he finds Jesse, father of eight boys. *Eight!*

Jesse presents his boys to Samuel to see if one is worthy to be king—starting with the oldest and biggest, naturally. Samuel looks at each and then asks Jesse if he's sure he doesn't have any more sons, since none of the initial seven presented were chosen.

It's almost as if Jesse forgot he had an eighth son. Or perhaps he didn't think it was worth it to present David; after all, he is the youngest and he's *just* a shepherd. But these words spoken by the Lord to Samuel tell us everything we need to know about underestimating people: "Do not look at his appearance or his stature . . . for humans see what is visible, but the LORD sees the heart" (v. 7 CSB).

As soon as David is presented to Samuel, God makes it clear that David is the chosen one. Samuel anoints David, and the Spirit of the Lord comes powerfully on him. From there, David goes on to defeat Goliath and one day becomes king.

No one thought that young David, the poet out tending sheep in the pasture, would be the next king of Israel. He was underestimated, but it didn't matter because God had a different plan.

There will be times when you will be underestimated as well. People will think you don't have what it takes.

But your potential is not measured by their perceptions. When you lean into what you were created to do and allow the Spirit of the Lord to work powerfully within you, there's no telling what might happen.

Underestimating people is really underestimating what God can do in people. Since we serve a great and powerful God who can work through anyone, we better stop underestimating and start prayerfully considering how we will participate in the work God is doing!

READING GOD'S WORD

But the LORD said to Samuel, "Have no regard for his [Eliab's] appearance or stature, because I haven't selected him. God doesn't look at things like humans do. Humans see only what is visible to the eyes, but the LORD sees into the heart." (1 Samuel 16:7)

[Jesus said,] "Consider a mustard seed. When scattered on the ground, it's the smallest of all the seeds on the earth; but when it's planted, it grows and becomes the largest of all vegetable plants. It produces such large branches that the birds in the sky are able to nest in its shade." (Mark 4:31–32)

REFLECT AND RESPOND

Journaling Questions

Have you ever been underestimated? How did that experience make you feel?

David was underestimated when he went to face Goliath. To the naysayers he said, "Your servant has fought both lions and bears. . . . The LORD . . . who rescued me from the power of both lions and bears, will rescue me from the power of this Philistine" (1 Samuel 17:36–37). What would it look like for you to have this kind of confidence in the Lord's help?

How might knowing that God has a direction for your life help you have confidence when you feel underestimated by others?

Pray This Prayer

God, there have been times I've felt underestimated. There will be more times when I feel underestimated in the future. When those situations come up, remind me that my worth and potential come from you. Help me not to underestimate myself but to allow space for you to work powerfully in and through me. In Jesus' name, amen.

SOMETHING TO TRY

Are you feeling discouraged because someone has underestimated you? Write yourself a note reminding yourself how much God believes in you.

THE TAKEAWAY

Underestimating people is underestimating God. Believe God can work through you even when others—or you—don't believe it.

POST 10

Why Can't You Be Like Them?

Teri was leading the Christian Club at her school.

In comparison, I (Kara) was embarrassed to tell my friends that I was attending the Christian Club at my school.

Another close youth group friend, Julie, was always happy to help with any task. From picking up trash after events to stuffing envelopes for a church mailer, she stepped up to volunteer.

I usually held back from volunteering, hoping someone else would sign up first.

When I compared myself to Teri, I felt like a wimpy Christian. Next to Julie, I felt selfish.

All throughout high school, I wondered, *Why can't I be more like them? What's wrong with me that I can't share my faith like Teri and share my time like Julie?*

Like Me

Comparing ourselves to others is using the wrong yardstick. I'm not *supposed* to be just like Teri or Julie. I'm supposed to be *like me*. Like the me God has designed me to be.

Every human on the planet has gifts and talents given to them by God. Teri has the gift of sharing her faith (often called the gift of evangelism). Julie has the gift of service.

While I know God wants me to share my faith and time when I have the chance, I'll rarely do so as well, or as much, as Teri and Julie.

I've come to realize many of my gifts are connected to the gift of leadership. Those gifts are neither better nor worse than Teri's and Julie's; they are just different.

Paul writes to the church in Rome about their gifts, but it's not the only list Paul provides of possible gifts and skills. In 1 Corinthians 12:7–11, Paul adds more gifts—including the gifts of faith, healing, and wisdom. In Ephesians 4:11–13, Paul describes more roles—such as apostles, evangelists, and pastors.

You have gifts and passions that no one else does.

Your friends have talents that you don't.

We will better understand our identity when we discover the unique gifts and passions that God has given us and wants us to use to impact others around us!

READING GOD'S WORD

We have many parts in one body, but the parts don't all have the same function. In the same way, though there are many of us, we are one body in Christ, and individually we belong to each other. We have different gifts that are consistent with God's grace that has been given to us. If your gift is prophecy, you should prophesy in proportion to your faith. If your gift is service, devote yourself to serving. If your gift is teaching, devote yourself to teaching. If your gift is encouragement, devote yourself to encouraging. The one giving should do it with no strings attached. The leader should lead with passion. The one showing mercy should be cheerful. (Romans 12:4–8)

REFLECT AND RESPOND

Journaling Questions

> What are a few of your gifts or talents?

> When are you most likely to compare your gifts with the gifts of others? How does that comparison usually make you feel about yourself and the other person?

> During those times when you feel like your gifts aren't as good as the gifts of others, what do you think God would want you to remember about yourself?

Pray This Prayer

God, I love how you've given each of us gifts and talents, but I confess that sometimes I envy what you've given others. Please help me to be grateful for the gifts and passions you've given me. Please show me how to use them to help others and bring you glory. In Jesus' name, amen.

SOMETHING TO TRY

God doesn't want—or expect—us to figure out who we are on our own. God gives us community to help. If you have no clue what your gifts and talents are, try asking a few friends, teachers, people at church, or family members. If you have a hunch, run it by a few friends or adults who know you well.

Try using those gifts at church, in your youth group, with your friends, and at home. Pay attention—and talk—to adults who might have similar gifts as you and learn from them. Experiment, get feedback from others, and see what feels right.

THE TAKEAWAY

Let others' gifts and talents inspire you to figure out—and strengthen—your own!

POST 11

You Are More Than Your Failure

> I don't want to mess up, but I guess everyone has a fear of failure. So I feel like if I am failing or am not doing as great, I worry about it. I don't want to be all negative and just think that there is no way out, you know? I hate having that feeling of being stuck. And I think that's how everyone at my school feels.
>
> Daniel

Have you ever failed so hard or so badly you didn't know if you would be able to recover?

Maybe you failed a test or a class. Maybe you failed in a relationship. Maybe you failed to be admitted into a prestigious program. Maybe you simply failed to get up on time and missed the bus for school, just another failure in a long list of failures. No matter your failure, chances are you felt crushed.

Sometimes failure can feel like forever, like there can't be any redeeming quality to it. It's as if from now on, *failure* is who you are and nothing else matters.

We're all in danger of falling into this unhealthy pattern. We internalize this identity and can't see beyond it. But what if failure doesn't have to be the end? What if we can learn from our failures and move forward more informed and compassionate than before?

Failure Isn't the End

You can find great comfort in knowing that you are more than your failure because failure happens to everyone. We all experience it at one point or another, and yet, we almost always find a way to move on. When we see beyond a failure to the lesson learned or the opportunity gained, we begin to understand that failure is not the end; it's simply a new beginning.

Here's one truth we can hold on to in the midst of our failures: God is tenderly holding us even—maybe especially—when we fail. God is dusting us off and helping us back to our feet. We're not left behind, forgotten, or worthless.

Think of Peter, one of Jesus' disciples. We see in Scripture that he had plenty of failures, yet each time we see Jesus patiently and lovingly instructing him instead of rejecting him. One example is when the disciples witnessed Jesus walking on water. Peter decided to give it a try—and he was doing great! Until he took his eyes off Jesus and became fearful of all the waves. Soon he started to sink! But Jesus reached out his hand and rescued Peter. (Read the rest of the story in Matthew 14:22–33.)

When you experience a failure, you can imagine Jesus reaching out his hand to you as well. He will help you back up and help you to keep walking forward.

READING GOD'S WORD

A person's steps are made secure by the Lord
 when they delight in his way.
Though they trip up, they won't be thrown down,
 because the Lord holds their hand. (Psalm 37:23–24)

The Lord supports all who fall down,
 straightens up all who are bent low. (Psalm 145:14)

REFLECT AND RESPOND

Journaling Questions

When have you recently experienced failure? How did you feel in that moment?

What are some positive outcomes of failure?

What do you think God thinks of you when you fail? How might knowing what God actually thinks of you in the face of failure change the way you see yourself in your mistakes and missteps?

Pray This Prayer

God, failure often feels like an embarrassing end. It doesn't feel good. Sometimes I'm not even sure how to move past the failure. But no matter what, when I experience failure, I pray the Holy Spirit will remind me of my true identity as a beloved child of God. I am more than my failures, and I don't have to hide or feel ashamed. Thank you for approving of me and loving me before, during, and after I fail. In Jesus' name, amen.

SOMETHING TO TRY

Sometimes we fear failure so much that we don't even attempt certain tasks or activities. Think of a goal you can set or an activity you can try that you've been avoiding due to fear of failure. Tell someone about it and give it a try! Even if you fail, remember that you are more than your failure. In fact, sometimes the real failure is in choosing never to try! You're succeeding simply by taking the risk to start.

THE TAKEAWAY

Failure isn't just an end—it can be a beautiful beginning.

POST 12

You Are More Than Your Success

Pastor and author Tim Keller once said, "When work is your identity, if you are successful it goes to your head, if you are a failure it goes to your heart."[1]

I (Kristel) think about this a lot. The truth is, while failing is a difficult experience, sometimes it's success that really trips us up. Failure is humbling, but the danger of success is that it can fill us with pride. It can trick us into thinking we are great.

At least that's been my experience. Growing up, I was a good student. I often made the honor roll. I succeeded in music and writing. I went to college on a scholarship and went on to earn my master's degree. I didn't understand why other people couldn't get it together. Surely, success wasn't that hard. Look at me!

Then one day, I noticed anxiety creeping into my head and heart. With each new success, I would panic: *I have to keep this up. If I mess up, I won't be a success anymore and people will look down on me. I'll be laughed at. I'll be ridiculed. I won't have that perfect streak anymore. Who even am I if I'm not successful in this?*

Being a success had gone to my head and filled me with pride, but it had also made me terrified to fail. If I wasn't successful, then I was nobody.

More Than What You Produce

Here's the truth: You are more than what you succeed at or produce. You are a person, a beloved child of God. You don't gain value through your success; you already have value because God created you in God's own image.

The first time I had an epic fail, I was surprised at what happened next. *Relief* washed over me. I looked around and realized that the earth had not shattered. I was still me. Still loved. Still whole. Still valuable. The weight had been lifted from my shoulders as I realized I no longer had to keep up the façade of success.

Since I had made success my identity, I feared that failure would become my new identity. But all along, my true identity was in Jesus Christ. My identity isn't in what I do but in who I am.

In Christ, you are forgiven, loved, redeemed, chosen, victorious, and so much more. Don't settle for an identity built on what you do; you're so much more than that.

READING GOD'S WORD

> So then, if anyone is in Christ, that person is part of the new creation. The old things have gone away, and look, new things have arrived! (2 Corinthians 5:17)

> The law of the Spirit of life in Christ Jesus has set you free from the law of sin and death. (Romans 8:2)

REFLECT AND RESPOND

Journaling Questions

> Do you struggle with remembering your identity is in Christ rather than in your success? If so, where do you think this struggle comes from?

What are some benefits of success? What are some dangers?

How can you remember who you are in the face of both success and failure?

Pray This Prayer

God, I don't want success to go to my head. Keep me humble by remembering that my identity is not in anything I do—my identity is rooted in Christ and secure in your love. Thank you for your unconditional love. In Jesus' name, amen.

SOMETHING TO TRY

Read the following verses and identify the words that call out who you are in Christ: John 1:12; Romans 8:37 (NIV); Galatians 3:26–29; Ephesians 2:10, 19; 1 Peter 2:9. Make a list of these words and keep it in your Bible for you to read through whenever you need a reminder.

THE TAKEAWAY

Your true identity is not in your success or in what you produce but has already been given to you by God.

POST 13

You Are More Than Your Stuff

Where do you have the most stuff?

It might be in your closet or drawers. It might be on your phone, your gaming device, an online world.

Maybe where you have the most stuff is where you have the most *actual* stuff or where you *care about* your stuff the most or where you *wish* you had more. Like having enough of the right kinds of shoes. Or taking enough photos of yourself looking a certain way.

Go there right now and take a look around. What do you notice? Think about where, when, and why you got all the things you have in that place now. What things could you do without? What are some things you wish were there?

How complicated has your life become as a result of your stuff? How much stuff do you really need?

Another Way

Whether you don't need everything you already have or you are struggling to get by, through Jesus' life you're invited to live another way. A way that isn't complicated by the fear and worries that we all know so well but is guided by this simple truth: *we can trust God, who knows us and knows our needs.*

You aren't defined by your stuff—neither physical possessions you've collected nor digital worlds you've constructed. Sometimes subtracting or simplifying can help you see yourself more clearly.

Now, this doesn't mean you have to live in the dark ages before smartphones, online shopping, or thrift store hauls. But you can probably afford to let go of some stuff in your life—especially stuff that makes you anxious or makes you feel less worthy of love and acceptance.

Simplifying helps us put our trust in God and realize that we are not at the mercy of the pressures and worries that swirl around us. And we might find space to see ourselves, God, and people in our world more clearly.

On the other hand, you also aren't defined by your *lack* of stuff. If you or your family is in need more often than not, the absence of material wealth has no claim on who you truly are. Jesus invites us to trust God whether we have enough or whether we're worried we may not, because God is our heavenly Father who thinks we are worth caring for.

READING GOD'S WORD

Therefore, I say to you, don't worry about your life, what you'll eat or what you'll drink, or about your body, what you'll wear. Isn't life more than food and the body more than clothes? Look at the birds in the sky. They don't sow seed or harvest grain or gather crops into barns. Yet your heavenly Father feeds them. Aren't you worth much more than they are? Who among you by worrying can add a single moment to your life? And why do you worry about clothes? Notice how the lilies in the field grow. They don't wear themselves out with work, and they don't spin cloth. But I say to you that even Solomon in all of his splendor wasn't dressed like one of these. If God dresses grass in the field so beautifully, even though it's alive today and tomorrow it's thrown into the furnace, won't God do much more for you, you people of weak faith? Therefore, don't worry and say, "What are we going to eat?" or "What are we going to drink?" or "What are we going to wear?" Gentiles long for all these things. Your heavenly Father knows that you need them. Instead, desire first and foremost God's kingdom and God's righteousness, and all these things will be given to you as well. Therefore, stop worrying about tomorrow, because tomorrow will worry about itself. Each day has enough trouble of its own. (Matthew 6:25–34)

REFLECT AND RESPOND

Journaling Questions

What do you notice about Jesus' words? What do you think it means to "stop worrying about tomorrow, because tomorrow will worry about itself" (v. 34)?

Take a look at your stuff again. Do you have enough? More than enough? If you made a list of what is really important, would all this stuff make the list?

Pray This Prayer

Lord, free me from the deceptive lure of stuff. Remind me over and over that my value isn't based on what I gather, own, or build but on what you've already determined my worth to be. In Jesus' name, amen.

SOMETHING TO TRY

Pick one thing—physical or virtual—to subtract this week. Choose something that makes you feel less than enough or that raises your anxiety or that is just cluttering your life in some way. After a week, evaluate how you feel and ask yourself whether you can live without it altogether.

THE TAKEAWAY

You are so much more than what you have.

POST 14

You Are a Child of God

Throughout the pages of this portion of the book, you will notice three words we come back to often: *child of God*.

These words are not simply a cute catchphrase or an empty platitude—they are words bursting with deep meaning.

What does it mean to be a child of God?

First, it means God created us. In Genesis, we learn that God created humans with love and intentionality. God desires to have a relationship with us. We are made in the image of God, which gives us inherent value and worth.

Second, we read in Ephesians 1:5 that although sin separates us from God, we are offered an opportunity to join God's family through adoption because of Jesus. It was God's loving plan that we would be united with God forever.

Third, we are transformed into new creations. Second Corinthians 5:17 says we are made new. We are given a new nature. It's because of this new nature that we begin to experience transformation in our thoughts and actions. Little by little, we take on God's family resemblance.

Fourth, we have direct access to God, who loves us and supplies all our needs. We can trust God to care for us just as good parents care for their children. We do not need to fear coming before God, our perfect parent—instead, we are invited into God's family.

Finally, we can be confident that God will stick it out with us and that eventually we'll be together face-to-face: "And I am certain that God, who began the good work within you, will continue his work until it is finally finished on the day when Christ Jesus returns" (Philippians 1:6 NLT).

Wow. That's a lot!

Realizing all that it means to be a child of God can be overwhelming, but don't be afraid. It's with so much love that you're called God's child.

Every other identity you hold on to is second to this.

When you view life through this lens, everything changes.

READING GOD'S WORD

> God destined us to be his adopted children through Jesus Christ because of his love. This was according to his goodwill and plan. (Ephesians 1:5)

> There is neither Jew nor Greek; there is neither slave nor free; nor is there male and female, for you are all one in Christ Jesus. (Galatians 3:28)

REFLECT AND RESPOND

Journaling Questions

> What are some identity markers you have been building your life on?

What does it mean to make *child of God* your primary identity?

How might making that the most important part of your identity change how you think about your life and relationships?

Pray This Prayer

God, when I begin to forget, remind me that I am a child of God. This is my primary and most important identity. Thank you for making me and calling me your own. I trust in you to care for me and provide for all my needs. In Jesus' name, amen.

SOMETHING TO TRY

Use a dry-erase marker to write "Child of God" on your mirror at home. See this as a daily reminder of who you are.

THE TAKEAWAY

Whoever else you may be, your first identity is *child of God.*

POST 15

Unplugging to Notice God

I (Brad) will start this one with a confession.

I am really easily distracted. My brain randomly jumps from one thing to the next, and scrolling on my phone amps that up big-time. Sometimes I leave my phone in another room on purpose so I can focus—or just take a break.

Maybe you can relate. So today we're going to do something a little different. First, find somewhere you can be quiet and still for a little while. Turn off your devices and begin to settle down. Close your eyes and take a deep breath.

Think of all the distractions in your life—the things that cause you anxiety, fear, or stress. Imagine these things written on wet sand at the beach.

Now imagine the ocean tide sweeping in and completely erasing the words, leaving behind a smooth surface.

Sit in a moment of silence, letting the waves wash over your distractions when they try to take over. Take a couple of deep breaths. Invite God's Holy Spirit to be with you in that silence.

Being Still in a Distracted World

Unplugging from distractions can be tough. Most of us push pretty hard through our days, and we fill the empty spaces with our screens—to catch up, stay connected, play games, and sometimes just because we're used to looking down when we have a free minute. All this leaves us overwhelmed with life's distractions, even when we don't realize we're overwhelmed.

That's why we need to stop and breathe every now and then. Because sometimes it takes being still to settle down—and sometimes that's what it takes to notice God.

Now that you've taken a minute to get quiet, you're going to read Scripture as a way to notice God using a pattern that involves four steps: *Read*, *meditate*, *pray*, and *contemplate*. We'll walk through them together.[1]

The first step is to *read* the passage. As you read, take note of any words or phrases that stick out to you. Read slowly, maybe even reading it through a few times.

Next, *meditate* on the word or phrase you noticed most. Focus in on it for a few minutes. Make a list or draw some images of other things that are similar to this word or phrase. Why do you think this grabbed your attention?

Then *pray*. Invite God to speak to you about your own life in light of this passage—about who you are and what's going on with you. Talk to God about what's on your heart and mind right now.

Finally, *contemplate*. Just sit with your thoughts. Don't rush out of this moment. Take a few more slow breaths.

Ready? Let's give it a try.

READING GOD'S WORD

God is our refuge and strength,
  a very present help in trouble.
Therefore we will not fear, though the earth should change,
  though the mountains shake in the heart of the sea;
though its waters roar and foam,
  though the mountains tremble with its tumult. . . .

"Be still, and know that I am God!
  I am exalted among the nations,
  I am exalted in the earth."

The Lord of hosts is with us;
the God of Jacob is our refuge. (Psalm 46:1–3, 10–11 NRSV)

REFLECT AND RESPOND

Journaling Questions

What is easy and what is hard about putting distractions aside for a little while?

What are the quietest parts of your day? What do you tend to do when you have a quiet moment to yourself?

When and where do you notice God most in your life? Through quiet? Scripture? Prayer? Being outside? Being with people? Singing? Consider what helps you best connect with God's Spirit.

Pray This Prayer

God, I go through my days so distracted. There's so much noise all around me—and inside me. Teach me to practice quiet, to practice stillness, and to find ways to unplug from all the distractions in order to notice you more. As I do, show me more about who I truly am. In Jesus' name, amen.

SOMETHING TO TRY

Sometime this week, repeat this pattern: *read*, *meditate*, *pray*, and *contemplate* with this passage or another one (maybe read all of Psalm 46 or pick another psalm—there are 150 of them!).

Consider something you could "unplug" from for a while to create space to notice God. This doesn't need to be something that literally plugs in (like a computer or phone, although those are options). It could be any of life's distractions. Take a moment to think this over and write something you want to unplug from and how often or how long you want to unplug from it.

THE TAKEAWAY

When you make yourself still, there's more room to notice God.

POST 16

Faith and Anxiety

Janelle is an eleventh grader who has been diagnosed with generalized anxiety disorder. She first began struggling with anxiety in middle school:

> I didn't know it was anxiety at the time. I was always sick, but I would pretend I was fine, like there was nothing wrong. My therapist now says it was a coping skill. I wouldn't let myself eat if I was anxious. I would tell my mom that I had already eaten so she wouldn't be worried. Or I would tell her that I had friends I would hang out with, because I didn't want her to be worried that I wasn't making friends. I would hide in the bathroom to cry several times a day, and sometimes have panic attacks.

Now Janelle goes to therapy and takes medication to help. While Janelle openly discusses her ongoing journey with mental health and the fears she must battle in her mind, she also loves reading and working with kids. She excels at school and has a good home support system. There's more to her than just anxiety.

Not every teen has a diagnosable disorder, but almost every teen feels stressed regularly. When that stress begins to creep in, how do you respond? What role does faith play in the anxiety that often looms over your days?

Sometimes we feel anxiety when our perspective is skewed. We begin to feel overwhelmed by life, and we worry how we will get through it all. And rightfully so! Life is absolutely overwhelming at times. When our schedules get packed, when circumstances outside our control occur, when deadlines and tests approach—these can all be anxiety-inducing.

Peace Is a Person

But what if we took a different angle?

We know that life is full of trials—unexpected twists and turns. We know there is so much that is out of our hands. We know our weaknesses and that we are ill-equipped for some of the curveballs life throws at us.

But we also know this: we serve a big God who is with us at every mountaintop and in every valley.

Throughout life, we will face circumstances that could cause stress or anxiety, but God assures us that peace can be ours. Peace isn't about being surrounded by calm conditions; peace is a person, and his name is Jesus. We can place our trust in him.

Does this mean we don't need therapy or medication or other support at times to help us manage anxiety? Absolutely not. These are good tools that are available to us. Just like other organs, the brain is an organ that sometimes needs medicine. There is no shame in getting help. Therapy and medication can put us on the path to healing. But while we walk through adversity, God will also grow and develop our faith.

We are marked not primarily by stress and anxiety but by faith in the God who gives us peace.

READING GOD'S WORD

Rejoice in the Lord always. I will say it again: Rejoice! Let your gentleness be evident to all. The Lord is near. Do not be anxious about anything, but in every situation, by prayer and petition, with thanksgiving, present your requests to God. And the peace of God, which transcends all understanding, will guard your hearts and your minds in Christ Jesus. (Philippians 4:4–7 NIV)

> Whenever I'm afraid,
> I put my trust in you. (Psalm 56:3)

REFLECT AND RESPOND

Journaling Questions

When have you struggled with anxiety? What did it feel like?

When you begin to struggle with anxiety, what can you do to face those feelings and move past them?

How might knowing that Jesus brings you peace change the way you respond to or deal with stress and anxiety in your life?

Pray This Prayer

God, fear and anxiety are part of life, but they don't have to define me. In Christ, I have peace that transcends fear. I place my trust in you to walk me through every storm of life. I am glad you are always with me. In Jesus' name, amen.

SOMETHING TO TRY

When you begin to feel anxious, an immediate and simple action you can take is to perform some breathing exercises.

Let's try a breathing exercise right now.

1. Find a comfortable position. You can be sitting, standing, or lying down.
2. Close your eyes and relax your shoulders.
3. Breathe in through your nose for four seconds and hold it for two seconds.
4. Breathe out through your mouth for six seconds.
5. Try doing this for two to five minutes.

Take note of how you feel once you complete the breathing exercise. Next time you start to feel anxious, remember these steps.

THE TAKEAWAY

When anxiety creeps in, we can respond with faith because the God of peace is with us in every trial.

POST 17

Your Voice Matters

"I volunteer as tribute!"[1]

These were the words Katniss Everdeen screamed when her little sister was selected for the Hunger Games. In the fictional world of Panem, people weren't allowed to use their voices, especially the children who were being sent to these cruel games. These four words were the only way Katniss could use her voice to save her sister. Her voice may not have ever mattered before this moment, but when she discovered the power of her voice, it set her on a course to mobilize an uprising and save an entire country.

Like Katniss, you have a voice and your voice matters. *The Hunger Games* may not be your reality—you may not be the face of a revolution—but you have influence, no matter how big or small.

What will you do with your voice?

Gift and Responsibility

First, recognize that your voice is a gift from God. Think about it. First Corinthians 4:7 says that everything we receive is from God. This leads to two responses: *gratitude* for the gift of having a voice and *humility* because it's not our own doing, but God's. God gives you your voice, and it's given for a reason.

In *The Hunger Games*, Katniss uses her voice to save her sister. She goes on to use her voice to move the citizens of Panem to rise up against their oppressive and corrupt government. Basically, she uses her voice for those who have been silenced.

You also have a responsibility to speak up for others. This is one of the reasons your voice matters. Your voice is specific to you and can be helpful to many. No one else has *your* voice.

What is something you know about? What is something you're passionate about? Who is someone you can help? How can you use your voice to speak up? These are questions you can ask yourself as you figure out how to use your voice.

Don't waste time wondering if your voice matters; choose to believe the truth that it does, and then use it. Chances are someone is counting on you to use your voice, and they'll be glad when you do.

READING GOD'S WORD

Don't let any foul words come out of your mouth. Only say what is helpful when it is needed for building up the community so that it benefits those who hear what you say. (Ephesians 4:29)

> My mouth will proclaim the LORD's praise,
> and every living thing will bless God's holy name forever and always. (Psalm 145:21)

> After that I will pour out my spirit upon everyone;
> your sons and your daughters will prophesy,
> your old men will dream dreams,
> and your young men will see visions. (Joel 2:28)

REFLECT AND RESPOND

Journaling Questions

> Do you believe your voice matters? If not, what is stopping you from grasping hold of this truth?

> How can you use your voice to speak up for others?

Pray This Prayer

God, thank you for giving me a voice. I may shake when I use it, but I pray that you would empower me to use it nonetheless. Help me to see how I can use my voice to help others and bring glory to your name. In Jesus' name, amen.

SOMETHING TO TRY

This week, we have two options to try based on your comfort level.

Option 1: Take an index card and write down these words: "I am who God says I am. I am important. My voice matters, and I am deeply loved." Recite them each time you become uncertain about whether your voice matters.

Option 2: Post a video on social media using your voice to share about something that's important to you and advocate on behalf of someone else.

THE TAKEAWAY

Your voice matters because it is a gift from God to be used for a purpose.

POST 18

What's More Important Than What You See in the Mirror?

I (Kara) am about to share with you something that's pretty embarrassing.

In ninth and tenth grade, I kept a list of the clothes I wore each day to school.

I really cared about what I wore to school, and I didn't have a ton of clothes. Plus, I loved lists (and still do!). So I figured if I kept a list of each day's outfit, I could make it through each week without repeating any of my pants, shirts, or sweatshirts.

I even kept track of whether I wore my white, teal-green, or lavender tennis shoes. (What can I say about those color choices? I was a teenager in the '80s!)

I'm guessing few (and maybe none) of you reading this are keeping a list of what you're wearing to school each day. But maybe like me, you're very focused on what you wear.

Or how your hair looks.

Or your makeup.

Or if you have enough shoes. Or the right pair.

Or the best brand, or fit, of leggings, joggers, or jeans.

Or the perfect cap.

Or how you look in the thousands of photos and videos on your phone.

It's normal to care about how you look on the outside.

Focus on the Inside

But here's a question I would ask you—and wish someone had asked me early in high school: In the midst of the time you spend on your appearance, how much time are you spending on your heart? On your character—and who you are on the inside?

In ninth and tenth grade, I gave a lot of thought to my external grooming and little attention to my internal growth.

That changed in eleventh grade. A new youth pastor came to our church, and he invited us to commit to spending time with God every day.

I decided to spend five to seven minutes each morning with God. That still wasn't as much time as I spent on my clothes, hair, and makeup, but at least it was something.

How did I spend those five to seven minutes? By reading a few verses from the Bible and writing down a few prayers. Something else changed too: I no longer wrote down my outfits. Of course, I still cared about how I looked, but I gave less of each day to those details.

Did I miss some mornings focusing time on God? You bet. Lots. Then I would try to either spend time with God that night or wake up a few minutes earlier the next morning so that I didn't skip two (or three) days in a row.

To be really clear, there's nothing magical about five to seven minutes or writing down prayers. I wanted to strengthen my relationship with God and my inner character, and that's what worked for me. A different approach might work better for you. But regardless of what you do or when you do it, find something you can do each day to focus on the inside and grow your soul.

READING GOD'S WORD

Let the words of my mouth
and the meditations of my heart
be pleasing to you,
LORD, my rock and my redeemer. (Psalm 19:14)

Now we see a reflection in a mirror; then we will see face-to-face. Now I know partially, but then I will know completely in the same way that I have been completely known. (1 Corinthians 13:12)

REFLECT AND RESPOND

Journaling Questions

In what ways do you tend to focus on your outward appearance?

What could you do as a regular practice to focus more on your inner growth?

Pray This Prayer

God, it's so tempting to focus more on what's on the outside than what's deep inside. Please show me the right balance between paying attention to how I look and growing my soul and character. Please show me what I can do to grow internally into who you've made me to be. In Jesus' name, amen.

SOMETHING TO TRY

Consider how you spent the majority of your time in the past day. How much time did you spend thinking about and working on your external appearance? How much time did you spend thinking about and working on your inner development? How do you feel about your answers? What would you like to do differently in the day ahead?

THE TAKEAWAY

You are so much more than what your reflection shows.

You Are Enough Because of Jesus

I am not enough.

We've all thought these words at one point or another. Sometimes we don't feel smart enough . . . or pretty enough . . . or funny enough . . . or popular enough.

Sometimes you look in the mirror and your not-enough-ness is so overwhelming that tears sting your eyes and your heart sinks to the pit of your stomach. When you feel like you're not enough, you begin to question everything—your capacity, your intellect, your worth.

Think about the area where you feel not enough. Something that makes you feel unqualified or not good enough. What emotions does it stir up? Shame? Embarrassment?

In 2 Corinthians 12, one of Paul's letters written to an early church, he writes that Jesus spoke to him about his weakness and said something profound: "My grace is enough for you, because power is made perfect in weakness" (v. 9).

Wait, what does that say about weakness again? That's right, God's power is made *perfect* in it. But how can that be? And what exactly does that mean?

Remember the story of Moses? Exodus 3 tells of his encounter with God through a burning bush. God called Moses to a big job: freeing the Israelites from their captivity in Egypt. Picture the scene: Moses talking to a burning bush, probably kind of freaking out about the entire situation, and then he's told to walk up to Pharaoh and say, "Let my people go." Just like that. Imagine the look of shock on Moses' face as he thought, *Who, me?!*

The thing is, Moses was not very good at speaking; he likely had a speech impediment. Yet, God was calling him to go to the pharaoh and demand the Israelites' freedom.

Moses questions God's decision to send him on this mission. Surely, there was someone younger, stronger, and more charismatic for the job. But that's not what God was looking for. God wanted Moses—in all his *weakness*. When Moses asks for some authority and assurance, God doesn't give him a pep talk. Instead, God says he will be with him: "I AM WHO I AM. This is what you are to say to the Israelites: 'I AM has sent me to you'" (v. 14 NIV).

God Meets Us in Our Weakness

It was never about Moses' power but God's. We will struggle with weakness, but God's strength is inexhaustible. We will never be enough on our own, but God—the great "I AM"—is always enough. When we let go of our feelings of inadequacy and take hold of the power God works in and through us, everything changes. God is enough on our behalf.

Moses didn't have to be the best speaker or the strongest warrior. He simply had to say yes to God's power, active even in Moses' own weakness. God worked miracles through Moses because he said yes.

Think again about your weaknesses. How can you trust God's strength to fill in for your weaknesses? How can you let go of any shame or embarrassment you feel so that you can be honest about your inconsistencies and depend on God to be your enough?

Once you begin to reframe your thinking about your weaknesses, you will begin to see how God makes them enough.

READING GOD'S WORD

[Jesus] said to me, "My grace is enough for you, because power is made perfect in weakness." So I'll gladly spend my time bragging about my weaknesses so that Christ's power can rest on me. (2 Corinthians 12:9)

[Jesus'] divine power has given us everything we need for a godly life through our knowledge of him who called us by his own glory and goodness. (2 Peter 1:3 NIV)

REFLECT AND RESPOND

Journaling Questions

Why do you think God chose Moses to free the Israelites? How can you relate to the story of Moses?

In what areas of your life do you feel like you're not enough?

What steps can you take this week to embrace your weaknesses and allow God's strength to be enough?

Pray This Prayer

God, so often I feel like I'm not enough, but the good news is that I don't have to be. Jesus came to earth, lived a human life, died, and conquered evil and even death so that I could have new life. Jesus is my enough, and I don't have to hide my weaknesses anymore. Instead, I can be honest and embrace them as your power works in and through me. Thank you for being my enough. In Jesus' name, amen.

SOMETHING TO TRY

Take the words from 2 Corinthians 12:9 and insert your name: *God's grace is enough for ________, because power is made perfect in weakness.* Write this phrase on a Post-it note and put it somewhere you will see it daily—your bathroom mirror, bedroom door, or inside your Bible. Each time you read it, thank God, whose power is made perfect in your weakness.

THE TAKEAWAY

Your weaknesses can become an opportunity for God to work powerfully in and through you—to be enough and to make you enough.

POST 20

Union with Christ

John 15:1–17 is one of my (Kristel's) favorite passages of Scripture. Maybe it's because I love plants, but I find the imagery of a vineyard to be beautiful. There is so much meaning behind these words from Jesus, but today I want to focus on one word in particular: *abide*.

Depending on which translation of the Bible you read, it may say *abide*, *remain*, or *stay*. Each of these words comes from the Greek word *meno*. I like to look up the meanings of the words in the original languages used in the Bible to help me understand what the writer was trying to convey.

Meno means "to continue to be present, to be held continually, to endure, to remain as one."

When Jesus commands us to abide, what he's really saying is to *be present* with him and *allow him to hold us*. At its core, this is what union with Christ means. We abide in Christ by faith, and he abides in us by his Spirit. We never have to fear that he will leave us because our union with Christ is forever.

God will always abide in us. God never turns away or forgets about us. God is always waiting for us to dwell in God's presence. It's in the presence of God that we can truly rest and be revived. It's where we find our true identity—who God made us to be.

That doesn't mean it's all sunshine and rainbows.

Being Tended

Have you ever taken care of a plant? Sometimes leaves turn yellow and they have to be pruned. Sometimes the plant needs more water or less water or more sun or less sun—and the only way to figure out what the plant needs is to slow down and take time to pay attention to the plant.

Like the plant, there will be times when you need to be pruned or maybe even repotted entirely. There will be times when you will have to slow down and pay attention to what you need. There will be times when you're not sure what's even wrong, but you won't have to figure it out alone.

Your union with Christ ensures that God is with you, guiding you, forming you, leading you, loving you. Union with Christ means that you are a new creation, powered by Christ's resurrection, living in the kingdom of the Spirit, connected directly to God, the vineyard keeper—where you are always in good hands.

READING GOD'S WORD

> I am the true vine, and my Father is the vineyard keeper. He removes any of my branches that don't produce fruit, and he trims any branch that produces fruit so that it will produce even more fruit. You are already trimmed because of the word I have spoken to you. Remain in me, and I will remain in you. A branch can't produce fruit by itself, but must remain in the vine. Likewise, you can't produce fruit unless you remain in me. (John 15:1–4)

> I have been crucified with Christ and I no longer live, but Christ lives in me. And the life that I now live in my body, I live by faith, indeed, by the faithfulness of God's Son, who loved me and gave himself for me. (Galatians 2:20)

REFLECT AND RESPOND

Journaling Questions

What are different ways you can abide in Christ?

Is there anything that needs to be pruned in your life? What is it? What would it take to cut it out or to be free from it?

How might staying connected to Christ help you in the pruning and growing?

Pray This Prayer

God, you promise that if I remain in you, you will remain in me. I know you are always faithful in your promises. Help me to dwell in your presence and not in anything else. In Jesus' name, amen.

SOMETHING TO TRY

Whether you have a green thumb or not, this week go to a local plant store or nursery to purchase a small plant. A sales associate may be able to help you pick out a plant that is suitable to your lifestyle (it's okay if you need something that's hard to kill!). Commit to caring for that plant, and use it as a spiritual practice to slow down and abide. As you care for the plant, allow God to care for you.

If this isn't an option for you, take time to notice the plants and trees that grow outside. Watch how they grow, change, and develop over time.

THE TAKEAWAY

Union with Christ means that God is always abiding in you; you abide also in Christ.

PART 2

WHERE DO I FIT?

The Big Question of BELONGING

> Stop walking through the world looking for confirmation that you don't belong. You will always find it because you've made that your mission. Stop scouring people's faces for evidence that you're not enough. You will always find it because that's your goal. . . . No one belongs here more than you.
>
> Brené Brown[1]

What does it feel like to live as if "no one belongs here more than you"? To know you are welcomed, accepted, and embraced as "one of us," no matter what?

I (Brad) often have to remind myself of this truth. As you'll read in part 2, I grew up feeling like an outsider, and as an adult, I still don't quite fit in most of the time. I find myself distant from other people's experiences, lifestyles, or choices.

But as I read Scripture and spend time with other Jesus followers, I counter my negative self-talk with this Christ-centered answer to the question, Where do I fit?

I belong WITH God's people.

God has created us to be in community WITH God and WITH others through Jesus. We don't have to earn love, acceptance, or our place in the body of Christ. We belong to God and to one another.

We are not alone. We are family.

What's more, our truest belonging is not dependent on the success or failure of others to live it out. It has already been decided by the unconditional love of God.

WITH is our core word for belonging because it symbolizes the heart of God to be near us, among us, and close to us as beloved children for whom God's heart beats. God is WITH us—no matter what.

Each post in part 2 explores a different angle of what it means to *belong* with God and one another. We hope you'll see one word underneath all the rest: WITH.

POST 21

Belonging to a Safe Space

> Your belonging is your safe place. . . . You just feel secure when you belong somewhere.
>
> Michael

Are there some places where you feel safer than others? Are there some people who make you feel safe?

Safety—especially feeling safe to be who you truly are—is an important aspect of belonging. In some ways, safety is core to the very meaning of belonging. It's a prerequisite.

Arthur, a senior living on the West Coast, can tell the difference in his behavior when he feels safe with those nearby: "I have two personalities. One is really loud—that's who I am during the week. One is really quiet. That is my actual personality. That's who I am at church. The only place I can really recover and trust myself is at church." Arthur talked about safety as a word that "kind of encompasses everything, because it is the one place I can return to and still be loved regardless of whatever I do, whatever I say."

The fact that Arthur has a safe place to belong helps him express himself freely.

Sebastian, an eleventh grader, experienced abuse at home. He painfully recalled how it made him feel: "Being abused by my dad made me want to question my belonging everywhere I went. I had to make sure this was a place I belonged and that these were people who actually accepted me for who I am, because he didn't accept me at all. Even now, if I'm going to be in a new environment, I have to first make sure they accept me."

Unfortunately, Sebastian's experience has caused him to be more guarded and unsure of his belonging. He needs to establish safety in order to be himself.

Hailey summed up belonging this way: "It's like not having to be fake around certain people, because if you're being fake that's not where you belong, you know?"

We Find Safety in God

Each of these teenagers has had different experiences with belonging and safety. What's been your experience? Perhaps you have a loving and accepting home environment. Perhaps you've found a safe place at your local church. Perhaps you're still searching for safety and unsure whom to trust.

Psalm 91 offers words of comfort for those of us who are searching for a safe place to belong. In this psalm, we are reminded that God is our refuge and shelter. God covers us, rescues us, and delivers us. While we can't be certain what will happen in our lives, we can have certainty and assurance that God is with us; God is the safe space we have been searching for.

READING GOD'S WORD

Living in the Most High's shelter,
camping in the Almighty's shade,
I say to the Lord, "You are my refuge, my stronghold!
You are my God—the one I trust!"

God will save you from the hunter's trap
and from deadly sickness.

God will protect you with his pinions;
 you'll find refuge under his wings.
 His faithfulness is a protective shield.
Don't be afraid of terrors at night,
 arrows that fly in daylight,
 or sickness that prowls in the dark,
 destruction that ravages at noontime. . . .

God says, "Because you are devoted to me,
 I'll rescue you.
 I'll protect you because you know my name.
Whenever you cry out to me, I'll answer.
 I'll be with you in troubling times.
 I'll save you and glorify you.
 I'll fill you full with old age.
 I'll show you my salvation." (Psalm 91:1–6, 14–16)

REFLECT AND RESPOND

Journaling Questions

What has been your experience with safety and belonging?

Where do you consider to be your safe space?

> Have you considered that God is a safe space for you? How does it feel to reflect upon God as a safe space for you?

Pray This Prayer

God, you are my refuge and my fortress. You are my God in whom I can trust. I will make my home in you and be reminded that in you I am safe to be me. In Jesus' name, amen.

SOMETHING TO TRY

In Psalm 91:14–16, what does God promise to the psalmist and to us? Write it down on a note card and keep it in your Bible as a reminder of how God is a safe space for you.

THE TAKEAWAY

We belong when we feel safe. In God, we are always safe.

POST 22

What Do Real Friendships Look Like?

Susan B. Anthony and Elizabeth Cady Stanton met in 1851 in Seneca Falls, New York. At that time, women in the US didn't have many rights, including the right to vote. They wanted to change that. The two women led the way for the women's rights movement in the US.

They became fast friends through their shared passion for equality. Stanton had a gift for vision casting, writing, and speaking. Anthony had a gift for organizing and strategizing. Together they launched a national movement and published a newspaper called *The Revolution*. They were doing some really gutsy things!

Stanton and Anthony didn't always agree on how to fight for women's equality, and yet, they remained friends. They didn't allow disagreements to hinder their relationship. While they debated many things, they stayed united on the basics.

In 1902, Anthony wrote to her friend Stanton, "It is fifty-one years since we first met, and we have been busy through every one of them, stirring up the world to recognize the rights of women."[1] In another letter, Stanton wrote, "No power in heaven, hell or earth can separate us, for our hearts are eternally wedded together."[2]

Lessons in Friendship

These two women truly shared an inspirational friendship. Here are three ways their example can shape our own friendships today.

1. *Collaboration over competition.* When you have shared passions or goals with a friend, it becomes all too easy to compete against each other. Real friends know that they're better together. Rather than compete for opportunities, how can you join forces to bring about greater change? Learn to celebrate and collaborate rather than compete.
2. *Respectful disagreement.* There's no one in this world you will agree with 100 percent of the time. Friends will often disagree or have differing ideas. Being able to discuss different opinions without letting them get in the way of a personal relationship is key.
3. *Communication and connection.* Sometimes friends move away or go through seasons when they don't get to connect as regularly. Keep your friendships alive even if you are miles apart or on differing schedules. Keep each other up to date on your lives and show appreciation for one another. Sometimes we take friendships for granted, but we can make a huge difference when we remind those who are important to us how much we love and appreciate them.

The Bible talks about unity and love all through its pages. When there is mutual love, care, and respect in a friendship, you know it's on a good track.

READING GOD'S WORD

How good and pleasant it is
when God's people live together in unity! (Psalm 133:1 NIV)

> Friends love all the time,
> and kinsfolk are born for times of trouble. (Proverbs 17:17)

REFLECT AND RESPOND

Journaling Questions

What friendships do you admire? What do you admire about them?

Of the characteristics we talked about here (collaboration over competition, respectful disagreement, and communication and connection), which is easiest for you in friendship? Which is the most difficult?

What does it look like for you to be a good friend to someone this week?

Pray This Prayer

God, thank you for friends. It is comforting to know that I can have people to share my life with. Help me to be the type of friend you call us all to be. Help me to pursue love and unity in each of my friendships, and please bring friends into my life who strive for the same. In Jesus' name, amen.

SOMETHING TO TRY

Who is one of your good friends? Call, send a text, or write a letter reminding them how much you appreciate their presence in your life.

THE TAKEAWAY

Real friendships are based in mutual love, care, and respect. It's never a bad time to let your friends know you appreciate them.

POST 23

What Does It Mean for God to Be Your Friend?

> God is someone you love, who you have faith in, regardless if you can see him or not. God is that person who will always be there for you. God is our friend, our Father—our best friend actually. Once you start talking to him you feel his presence and know he's there, you know he's listening to you. God is that person you can't live without.
>
> Armando

The way we view God will shape our relationship with God.

God is described in multiple ways in the Bible—Lord, Almighty, Creator, Protector, Father, Mother, Spirit. Here's one you may not think of often: Friend.

It's true! You were made for friendship with God. God desires to have a relationship in which you *know* God, not just *know about* God. God wants to cultivate a real friendship, not just tell you what to do.

The night before Jesus went to the cross, he gathered with his closest companions, his disciples. Before they ate one last meal together, Jesus washed their feet as a symbol of humility and love. Then he began to give them his final teaching about truth and life. He told them he would not leave them alone and encouraged them to love one another.

And then he said, "I don't call you servants any longer, because servants don't know what their master is doing. Instead, I call you friends, because everything I heard from my Father I have made known to you" (John 15:15).

Jesus proved his friendship by being open and transparent. He withheld nothing from his disciples—or from us since we still have access to his words today.

Earlier in the conversation, Jesus said, "No one has greater love than to give up one's life for one's friends" (v. 13). The next morning when Jesus was crucified, the impact of those words must have pierced the hearts of the disciples.

Truly Jesus was their friend and is now our friend. He made the ultimate sacrifice when he laid down his life so that we could be restored to our full humanity and reconciled to God forever.

Developing a Friendship with God

Now that Jesus has opened the door to friendship with God, how do you develop this friendship? The same way you develop most friendships—through vulnerability, communication, and spending time together.

First, open your heart to God. As scary as that may seem, this is actually the safest your heart will ever be. God will tenderly hold your heart because God already knows and loves you.

Second, communication is key to any relationship. Imagine having a friend who never actually speaks to you. That would be weird! You can talk to God any time through prayer. God is always available and accessible.

Third, spending time with friends is important. Just like you want to spend time with your friends, God wants to spend time with you. You can do this by reading the Bible, praying, meditating, and worshiping. Setting aside intentional time with God will help you get to know God's heart.

READING GOD'S WORD

I don't call you servants any longer, because servants don't know what their master is doing. Instead, I call you friends, because everything I heard from my Father I have made known to you. (John 15:15)

Look! I'm standing at the door and knocking. If any hear my voice and open the door, I will come in to be with them, and will have dinner with them, and they will have dinner with me. (Revelation 3:20)

REFLECT AND RESPOND

Journaling Questions

Have you ever thought of God as your friend? How does that make you feel?

How does God show friendship toward us?

Which of these three things do you want to try in your friendship with God this week:

- Opening your heart?
- Communicating?
- Spending time together?

Pray This Prayer

God, you are my friend. Even if that doesn't always feel natural to say, it is the truth! Thank you for your loving friendship. Thank you for seeing me and pursuing a relationship with me. May I be open to pursuing a relationship with you as well. In Jesus' name, amen.

SOMETHING TO TRY

Dedicate a few minutes at the start or end of each day for a week to read the Bible and pray. At the end of the week, journal how your friendship with God has developed during that time. Eventually, you may be ready to increase the amount of time you spend with God each day.

THE TAKEAWAY

God desires a deep, genuine friendship with you.

POST 24

When You Feel Like an Outsider

> You want to know if you really fit in there, if they really like you coming along or just invited you because they felt bad.
>
> Janelle

I've always been a visitor in suburbia.

Let me (Brad) explain. My entire life, I've lived either on a farm or in a city. I've visited suburbs and have friends in suburbs, but I have never lived there.

This may sound silly. But sometimes when I'm with people, I can't relate to things they talk about. I've never had a garage with space to keep stuff like coolers or camping equipment. I don't own a lawn mower or a leaf blower.

I grew up driving tractors and working with cows and sheep, but I don't fit in with that lifestyle these days. And in the part of the city where I live now, I'm in the racial minority. I have had to learn a lot about the cultures of my neighbors to understand them, but I don't quite fit here either.

These parts of my life have all shaped my experiences of belonging. Feeling a little—or a lot—like an outsider has been part of my story.

Maybe you have different reasons for feeling as if you're on the outside. Maybe you live in a neighborhood where your family doesn't seem to have as much as some of the people around you.

Maybe you are a different race or come from a different ethnic background than most people at your school or church—or both.

Maybe you don't fit some of the stereotypes people expect of your gender.

Maybe the lunch you take to school seems weird to other kids, and you get embarrassed about your family's food.

Maybe you don't watch the same shows, listen to the same music, or follow the same influencers, so you're the only one who doesn't get the joke.

On some level or another, we've all experienced not belonging or only half belonging. We have felt on the edge of outside, half-included but not really "in."

No Outsiders

This may sound surprising to you, but Jesus understands what it's like to be on the outside.

He grew up normal in some ways but strange in others. He was a child refugee who grew up to live as a migrant. He chose to spend time with people on the margins—people others ignored. This made him fit in even less with all the "right" people—or anyone at all.

To make matters worse, his family struggled to understand him. In the end, his closest friends deserted him and he died a criminal's death, rejected by his own ethnic group and especially by the religious leaders. Ironically, God in the flesh was rejected and killed by the people whose job was to point to God.

Jesus didn't fit their categories. He was an outsider.

That's good news for us. Jesus took on all the awkwardness, shame, and loneliness of outsiders so he could identify with us—so his Godness could fully experience our humanness—and to welcome us to belong to him.

Jesus' welcome means there are no outsiders. We're all in. We all belong.

READING GOD'S WORD

You are all God's children through faith in Christ Jesus. All of you who were baptized into Christ have clothed yourselves with Christ. There is neither Jew nor Greek; there is neither slave nor free; nor is there male and female, for you are all one in Christ Jesus. (Galatians 3:26–28)

REFLECT AND RESPOND

Journaling Questions

When, where, or with whom do you feel like an outsider? What do you do when you don't fit in?

What are some things you and your friends do that might make other people feel like they don't fit in?

How might knowing you're always in—you always belong—with Jesus change the way you feel about where you fit? How might it change the way you treat or include others?

Pray This Prayer

Lord, sometimes I feel so lonely, even when I'm with other people. I question my belonging. Other people make me feel left out by the things they say and do, and I make myself feel like an outsider because of my own self-doubt. Give me courage to believe that you've erased all the reasons I don't belong. In Jesus' name, amen.

SOMETHING TO TRY

Take the next five minutes (set a timer if it's helpful) to close your eyes and imagine Jesus speaking to you, "You belong." One by one, picture all the places you feel like an outsider, and imagine Jesus speaking these words in each setting. Then just sit with that phrase quietly. Repeat whenever you need the reminder!

THE TAKEAWAY

Next time you feel on the outside, remember that Jesus has thrown out all the reasons you don't belong.

The Power of "With"

The New Testament opens with a story of an angel visiting a teenage girl and giving her a shocking message. We retell this story every year leading up to Christmas because it's so profound.

When the angel of the Lord announced that Mary would give birth to the Son of God, this fulfilled an Old Testament prophecy that said he would be called *Emmanuel*, which means "God with us."

God with us.

Think about that for a second. God is often portrayed as some far-off being, sitting in the heavenly realms, perhaps unaware or uninterested in our comings and goings. But that's not what the Bible says about our God. The Bible says that our God is *with* us. And with presence God brings security, love, assurance, grace, and so much more.

The Ministry of Presence

There is incredible power in being *with* one another. Sometimes we call that *the ministry of presence*. Have you ever been in a situation where you didn't want advice or opinions? Maybe you were going through a hard time and all you wanted was to sit in a room with your best friend. No talking. No questioning. No storytelling. You simply wanted to be with someone you could trust without having to explain anything.

There's comfort in the ministry of presence. It's uncomplicated, unassuming, and demands nothing.

Even Jesus, God with us, desired the ministry of presence with his closest friends. In Matthew 26, when facing the greatest trial of his life—going to the cross—Jesus asked the disciples to keep watch and pray. They could do nothing to change what was about to happen to him. He simply wanted their presence. And he returned the favor when, in Matthew 28, he said, "Look, I myself will be with you every day until the end of this present age" (v. 20).

The Holy Spirit is God's gift of presence to us now, and we can also be the flesh-and-blood gift of presence to one another in the name of Jesus.

Next time someone you know is dealing with a difficult circumstance, consider the power of "with" and how the ministry of presence can be a great comfort to them.

READING GOD'S WORD

> Look! A virgin will become pregnant and give birth to a son, and they will call him, *Emmanuel*. (*Emmanuel* means "God with us.") (Matthew 1:23)

> I heard a loud voice from the throne say, "Look! God's dwelling is here with humankind. He will dwell with them, and they will be his peoples. God himself will be with them as their God." (Revelation 21:3)

> The Word became flesh
> and made his home among us.
> We have seen his glory,
> glory like that of a father's only son,
> full of grace and truth. (John 1:14)

REFLECT AND RESPOND

Journaling Questions

When has someone's presence with you been comforting to you? What did they do? Did a friend sit with you while you were sad? Did a parent sit with you through difficult emotions?

What's so comforting about people being with you?

How can you show up and be present with someone in your life this week?

Pray This Prayer

God, you came near to be with us. You promised to be with us always. Thank you for showing us the power of the ministry of presence. As I go through my days, help me to recognize how I can be with people as well. In Jesus' name, amen.

SOMETHING TO TRY

Pray for an opportunity to practice the ministry of presence—the chance to be with someone. Ask God to open your eyes to who around you may need to experience the power of "with." When the opportunity arises, don't shy away from it, and resist any temptation to fix, explain, or ask questions. Simply be *with* the person who needs it.

THE TAKEAWAY

There is power in simply being with people—*the ministry of presence.*

Who God Is Reveals What Belonging Looks Like

Father, Son, and Holy Spirit. In the church, we call this the Trinity.

The Trinity can be, well, complicated. Basically, God is one essence expressed in three persons. Many have tried to use illustrations to explain the Trinity—from the three parts of an egg (shell, egg white, and yolk) to the states of water (solid, liquid, and gas).

None of these illustrations, however, fully explain the Trinity. So don't worry if it's confusing to you; the Trinity is a mystery to us all.

But have you ever wondered how the three persons—Father, Son, and Spirit—relate to one another?

One prayer of the early church (recorded in 2 Corinthians 13:14) highlights three aspects of God's character revealed in the three persons of the Trinity: grace, love, and fellowship. These traits of God are key to God's internal unity.

You see, God the Father, God the Son, and God the Holy Spirit are equal and eternal parts of the Trinity, but they are all distinctly unique parts. They each have a specific role and function. The Father creates, the Son redeems, and the Holy Spirit sets apart and empowers. Yet, in some mysterious and beautiful way, they cooperate and are fully present with one another.

Though God is one, the Father and the Son enjoy mutual love and partnership in the Spirit. That's why the biblical author John can say, "God is love" (1 John 4:8). God is love because God extends and receives love within Godself. God is one, and God is also a community.

Out of Unity Comes Community

Now let's turn from God to us. What does all this mean for humans? We were born out of this loving unity among the Trinity. We were not created out of loneliness or need but out of divine love. We were created for community.

The three aspects of God's character shared earlier—grace, love, and fellowship—are also important traits of a connected community. For people to exist in harmony, we need to love one another, we need to extend grace and forgiveness, and we need to work to build camaraderie and intimacy in our relationships.

Just as the Father, the Son, and the Spirit belong to one another, so we belong to one another. Just as God exists in a community that fully supports and cooperates together, we were created to do the same.

What does it look like when we fully support and cooperate with one another as God's image bearers? That's true belonging.

READING GOD'S WORD

> May the grace of the Lord Jesus Christ, and the love of God, and the fellowship of the Holy Spirit be with you all. (2 Corinthians 13:14 NIV)

> This is why I kneel before the Father. Every ethnic group in heaven or on earth is recognized by him. I ask that he will strengthen you in your inner selves from the riches of his glory through the Spirit. I ask that Christ will live in your hearts through faith. (Ephesians 3:14–17)

REFLECT AND RESPOND

Journaling Questions

Why is community important?

Do you see grace, love, and fellowship displayed in your community? How so?

How can you extend grace, show love, and pursue fellowship in your community?

Pray This Prayer

God, you exist eternally as three persons in a loving community. Since we are created in your image, we, too, are created to belong to a loving community. I thank you that you do not leave us alone, but you have put it in our hearts to belong to one another. Help me to be a supportive, loving, grace-filled person in my community. In Jesus' name, amen.

SOMETHING TO TRY

Grace, love, and fellowship. Make a list of how you can show these traits of God to someone in your community. Commit to taking one idea from your list and acting on it this week.

THE TAKEAWAY

God created us to live in community just like God exists eternally in community: Father, Son, and Holy Spirit.

POST 27

Welcoming Like Jesus

The New Testament story of Matthew the tax collector is fascinating. Reading it through our modern lens, it's hard to understand why it was a big deal for Jesus to call on Matthew to follow him. But think of it this way: Who is someone our society sees as a despicable person?

Someone who sells out his own people. Someone who takes advantage of the poor. Someone whose actions are shockingly bad.

Back then, that someone was Matthew.

Tax collectors in biblical times were the worst kind of people. They were Jews who worked with the Roman government against their own community. They stole money and cared more about financial gain than anything else. They were distrusted by the other Jewish people and were not welcome in the temple, synagogues, or others' homes.

You would not want to make room at your table for these guys.

Jesus, however, saw something different in Matthew. Jesus saw Matthew's need for restoration and welcomed him to join in on the caravan of redemption.

God's Family Is for Everyone

Matthew's need for restoration is the same need that lives in us all. When Jesus was questioned about hanging out with Matthew, Jesus responded, "Healthy people don't need a doctor, but sick people do. I didn't come to call righteous people but sinners to change their hearts and lives" (Luke 5:31–32).

When Jesus looked at Matthew, he saw Matthew's sin not as a reason to stay away from him but as a reason to draw closer. That's how Jesus views all people. It's how Jesus views you.

What if we viewed people the same way Jesus did? What if we looked at people with compassion, love, and grace? Would we be welcoming too? Would we expand the circle to make room?

God's desire is for all people to be welcomed into God's family—and we're the ones doing the welcoming. We don't have to draw lines in the sand. We can look at people who are hated, forgotten, or marginalized by society and create a space of healing and restoration for them. We can, like Jesus, hang out in their homes and talk over dinner. We can share the hope of the gospel with them.

We can demonstrate that everyone has a place in God's family. Everyone belongs.

READING GOD'S WORD

> As Jesus continued on from there, he saw a man named Matthew sitting at a kiosk for collecting taxes. He said to him, "Follow me," and he got up and followed him. As Jesus sat down to eat in Matthew's house, many tax collectors and sinners joined Jesus and his disciples at the table. (Matthew 9:9–10)

REFLECT AND RESPOND

Journaling Questions

> When Jesus says it is the sick who need a doctor, what does he mean?

Who is hard for you to love or welcome?

What can you do this week to take a step toward welcoming that person in the way Jesus calls us to welcome?

Pray This Prayer

God, you desire for all to be welcomed into your family, including me. As I embrace this reality, help me also to embrace those around me and welcome them in. May I be a reflection of your love and grace. In Jesus' name, amen.

SOMETHING TO TRY

Look around at your school or neighborhood. Can you identify one person who may not feel welcome? Take one step toward them this week—say hi, learn their name, stop to talk, maybe even invite them to lunch or to hang out after school. Get to know them and allow them to get to know you.

THE TAKEAWAY

Jesus always wants us to expand the circle, to make room at the table for more—even those who don't seem like they deserve it.

POST 28

When Family Gets Complicated

> In our church, we all come from very different backgrounds, but we all still love each other. And we might argue sometimes, but at the end of the day, we are like a family.
>
> Natalie

My brother and I (Kara) knew we needed to pace ourselves. This was the first of two, or sometimes three, Thanksgiving meals we had to eat.

Usually we had "lunch" with our mom and stepdad.

A midafternoon "dinner" with our dad and stepmom.

And a final "dinner and dessert" with our grandparents.

That's a lot of turkey, mashed potatoes, and pumpkin pie in eight hours. If we consumed too much in the first or second meal and were full for the next meal, we risked offending that set of relatives.

On the continuum of divorced parents, mine actually got along pretty well. And yet, my brother and I still often felt the tensions of our parents' divorce.

We didn't talk about one parent in front of the other.

We downplayed—and sometimes even hid—clothes from shopping trips with one parent so we didn't hurt the other parent's feelings.

At every school or church event they both attended, we tried to give roughly equal time and attention to both sets.

No one ever told us these rules of being children of divorce. But even as young elementary school children, we picked up these communication dos and don'ts.

No Family Is Perfect

Maybe your parents are divorced and you can relate to what I navigated—and still navigate. Perhaps your parents' divorce has been a whole lot messier than mine.

It's possible that one of your parents has passed away.

Or you are being raised by a single parent and have little to no contact with the other parent.

It might be that you're living with a grandparent, caregiver, or guardian.

Maybe your parents live in the same home as you; they say they love each other, but they don't seem to like each other very much.

Or perhaps your family life is pretty good and healthy.

Families can be complicated, even when everyone's trying their best. While research tells us that family relationships are some of the most influential, no family is perfect. All of us have been loved imperfectly by parents or guardians who struggle a little or a lot. (Trust me, I'm a parent now, so I know this firsthand!)

The good news is that our church can make up for what's missing or flawed in the family that's raising us. One (from a long list) of the reasons that it's good to be in Christ-centered community is because *the church can become our functional family.*

Are you eager for some advice from a wise older adult but don't have much of a relationship with your grandparents? Chances are good there's someone in your church who'd love to give you input.

Do you need to know you're deeply loved but feel distant today from the people you live with? Make an extra effort to get close to your faith community so you can experience their love for you.

As we believe in Jesus, we become God's children. God becomes our heavenly parent. We are adopted into a family that isn't perfect, but it can help us see what's good about our original family and also help make up for what's tough or missing.

READING GOD'S WORD

> But those who did welcome him,
> those who believed in his name,
> he authorized to become God's children,
> born not from blood
> nor from human desire or passion,
> but born from God. (John 1:12–13)

> God destined us to be his adopted children through Jesus Christ because of his love. This was according to his goodwill and plan and to honor his glorious grace that he has given to us freely through the Son whom he loves. (Ephesians 1:5–6)

REFLECT AND RESPOND

Journaling Questions

> What do you appreciate about the family you're living with or who's raising you? What is sometimes tough about living with them?

> How does it make you feel to know that you belong to a family of believers?

> How can other followers of Jesus help make up for what's missing in the family that's raising you?

Pray This Prayer

God, I am grateful that you've designed us to be in close relationship with others. While the family I live with isn't perfect, I thank you that you've also given me a family of other imperfect Jesus followers. Please show me who in God's family I can go to for support as well as who I can tangibly care for and build up. In Jesus' name, amen.

SOMETHING TO TRY

What type of connection or care do you most need from your church family these days? What other teenager(s) or adult(s) in your church or faith community could offer you that care? Which adults can you go to with your questions or struggles when you don't feel comfortable going to your parents?

Reach out to those adults—by text, phone, email, or social media—and try to get that support. Be open to how God might want to use you to support or build up others in your church family too.

THE TAKEAWAY

Whether our home life is strong or struggling, God has given us a faith family too.

POST 29

How to Be a Peacemaker

By now, you've probably studied apartheid in school. *Apartheid* was the system of institutionalized racial segregation in South Africa that lasted from the late 1940s to the 1990s. Nonwhites in South Africa experienced discrimination on a grand scale during this time. Tension constantly ran high.

People of color had the laws stacked against them simply for the color of their skin. Some felt mad. Others hopeless. Some tried to fight back, while others resigned themselves to the status quo. If you've experienced racism or other kinds of prejudice, then you know the complicated feelings that can follow. If you haven't, try putting yourself in the shoes of someone who has.

Desmond Tutu was a South African Anglican bishop—a Black man, serving and ministering in the heart of South Africa. He came from a poor background and experienced hardship. Despite this, he pursued theological studies and rose through the ranks of the Anglican Church.

However, Bishop Tutu was not blind to the damage racist apartheid laws were causing in his country. He knew he had to do something, but what? What could a bishop do to create change? Aren't Christians told to be peacemakers? You can't really stir up change if you're trying to keep the peace, can you?

Peacekeeper vs. Peacemaker

We must make an important distinction between peace*keeping* and peace*making*. Peacekeepers walk on eggshells and avoid confrontation. They stick to the status quo and refuse to rock the boat—even if it means that injustices go unchecked.

Peacemakers, on the other hand, look confrontation square in the face and work toward change. Peacemakers try to unite people and create bridges of unity. Peacemakers are justice seekers.

Desmond Tutu was a peacemaker. He was committed to nonviolence but used his voice and influence to advocate on behalf of the Nonwhite population of South Africa. He raised money, supported civil rights work, testified before governments, made speeches, and never backed down from his belief that all people should be treated equally.

In 1984, Tutu was granted the Nobel Peace Prize. Then in the early 1990s, apartheid was finally officially dismantled.

What was the driving force behind Tutu's desire for equality? Read some of his words:

> Goodness is stronger than evil. Love is stronger than hate. Light is stronger than darkness. Life is stronger than death. Victory is ours through [God] who loved us.[1]

> If you want peace, you don't talk to your friends. You talk to your enemies.[2]

> There will be no future without forgiveness.[3]

> We have an extraordinary God. God is a mighty God, but this God needs you. When someone is hungry, bread doesn't come down from heaven. When God wants to feed the hungry, you and I must feed the hungry. And now God wants peace in the world.[4]

Desmond Tutu had experienced "vertical" reconciliation—peace with God. This led him to seek "horizontal" reconciliation—peace with the people around him. Without God, this peace would not have been achievable, but with God, victory was attainable. Maybe not in Tutu's lifetime or even ours, but someday.

READING GOD'S WORD

> Remember that once you were Gentiles by physical descent. . . . At that time you were without Christ. You were aliens rather than citizens of Israel, and strangers to the covenants of God's promise. In this world you had no hope and no God.
>
> But now, thanks to Christ Jesus, you who once were so far away have been brought near by the blood of Christ.
>
> Christ is our peace. He made both Jews and Gentiles into one group. With his body, he broke down the barrier of hatred that divided us. He canceled the detailed rules of the Law so that he could create one new person out of the two groups, making peace. He reconciled them both as one body to God by the cross, which ended the hostility to God.
>
> When he came, he announced the good news of peace to you who were far away from God and to those who were near. We both have access to the Father through Christ by the one Spirit. (Ephesians 2:11–18)

REFLECT AND RESPOND

Journaling Questions

> Why do you think vertical reconciliation with God leads to horizontal reconciliation with people?

Have you experienced peace with God? If not, what step can you take to experience that peace?

How can you be a peacemaker in your community?

Pray This Prayer

God, being a peacemaker is not easy. It's active and requires courage. Help me to be a peacemaker in my family, friend group, and community. Remind me that your Spirit empowers me to bring peace into every situation. In Jesus' name, amen.

SOMETHING TO TRY

Where do you see the need for peace in your world? In a friendship, a group at school, your family? How can you commit to making peace in that situation? Consider asking a trusted adult to help you.

THE TAKEAWAY

Vertical peace with God leads to horizontal peace with others—not because we're peacekeepers but because we're peacemakers.

POST 30

Why Authenticity Matters

> I let people know I'm a Christian, and sometimes I get that look like it's kind of surprising because they know Christians are judgmental and all that stuff. But I'm very welcoming, very open-minded and accepting of people. I feel like I have an obligation—not only for myself but for others—to show that being a Christian is not what they say, it is more of a community that loves one another no matter what; we are always there for you.
>
> Gabriel

I (Kristel) have always been the type of person who values authenticity—being real. The alternative seemed like too much to keep up with. I didn't want to be someone in one setting and a completely different person in another setting. I wanted to be *me*. This was especially true when I was a teenager. I wanted the freedom to be me in any setting and not be judged for it.

Most teens want to find relationships where they can be authentic. Garrison, a pastor in Tennessee who works with teenagers, said, "The search to belong is intersecting with current events and what's happening in a young person's life. I think the need for authenticity is heightened. . . . They want to share anger and frustration and confusion without someone trying to dictate how those emotions should be felt or expressed."

To really feel like you belong, you probably need to feel safe enough to be who you are and express yourself without being judged. I try to remember that now in my work with teens. I have a small group of young women I've been walking with since they were in middle school. Each time we meet, I remind them that this is a safe place for them to share. I tell each girl that I want to know her—the *real* her—and want her to know me and each of the others in the group for who we really are.

I've learned over the years that if you want someone to be authentic and vulnerable, often you must be willing to go first. So I share with them past and current struggles. I share my doubts and questions. I try to be open so we can find points of connection.

Now that my girls are in high school, we've lived through many ups and downs together. We've built trust with one another that's based in authenticity.

Authentic Faith

God also wants us to be authentic with our faith. I've heard people call Christians fake or hypocrites, but God calls us to have authentic faith. In James 2:14–26, the author criticizes Christians whose actions don't match up with their faith. You can't say you're a Christian in one setting but then behave in a way that doesn't represent Christ in another.

Why would James write something so harsh? Well, in his community, Christians were saying they followed Jesus but were talking bad about one another. Christians were saying they followed Jesus but weren't meeting the needs of the people in their community. Sound familiar? "My brothers and sisters, what good is it if people say they have faith but do nothing to show it? . . . Imagine a brother or sister who is naked and never has enough food to eat. What if one of you said, 'Go in peace! Stay warm! Have a nice meal!'? What good is it if you don't actually give them what their body needs?" (vv. 14–16).

People of faith care for one another. People of faith show love in tangible ways. This is the authentic faith to which we've been called.

READING GOD'S WORD

Someone might claim, "You have faith and I have action." But how can I see your faith apart from your actions? Instead, I'll show you my faith by putting it into practice in faithful action. (James 2:18)

REFLECT AND RESPOND

Journaling Questions

Why is authenticity an important characteristic?

Who is someone you can be authentic and vulnerable with?

How can you show others that they can be real with you?

Pray This Prayer

God, you value authenticity and desire for us to be authentic in every area of our lives. Help me to live out an authentic faith that loves and cares for people. In Jesus' name, amen.

SOMETHING TO TRY

On a piece of paper, write out James 2:18, but with your nondominant hand.

How does it feel? How does your handwriting look? Does it feel unnatural?

This is a physical representation of inauthenticity.

Now write the same verse with your dominant hand and notice how much better that feels. Reflect on how being authentic is really the most natural way to be.

THE TAKEAWAY

Authenticity lays the groundwork for belonging.

POST 31

How Can Empathy Fuel Belonging?

> Being heard is so close to being loved that for the average person, they are almost the same.[1]

Empathy is a word that gets thrown around a lot, but what does it really mean?

In its most basic sense, empathy is having the ability to understand and share the feelings of another person. To enter into their experience, and to try to see through their eyes and walk in their shoes for a little bit.

The Bible describes empathy in even simpler terms: "Be happy with those who are happy, and cry with those who are crying" (Romans 12:15).

Empathy is important in relationships. It's how we tell people that we notice and care about them. Empathy increases our desire to help others rather than ignore their pain. Empathy pushes past the superficial and creates a safe space for the real story to emerge.

Have you ever tried to communicate with someone, only to feel like they weren't really hearing you? Perhaps they weren't looking at you, distracted by another task. Or maybe they kept interrupting you, suggesting how you could fix the problem instead of simply listening. That's frustrating.

Listening Comes before Empathy

Feeling heard requires good listening. Listening brings us closer and sets the foundation for empathy. You cannot rejoice with someone if you don't know why they're rejoicing. You cannot cry with someone if you don't know why they're crying. Listening to what's going on and why is what makes empathy possible.

Rebekah is close to her mom and has learned the power of listening and empathy through that relationship. "When my mom hears what I'm going through, she says, 'I get it, I hear how you feel, that makes sense.'" Inspired by her mom's empathy and her small group leader's career as a therapist, Rebekah wants to be a counselor, creating a space of belonging for those who need it.

There is power in listening and empathy—it's the power of belonging. You can never truly belong in a place where you are not heard or cared for. If you want to be that safe place of belonging for someone, start by putting listening and empathy into practice.

READING GOD'S WORD

> Rejoice with those who rejoice; mourn with those who mourn. (Romans 12:15 NIV)

> Carry each other's burdens and so you will fulfill the law of Christ. (Galatians 6:2)

> If one part suffers, all the parts suffer with it; if one part gets the glory, all the parts celebrate with it. (1 Corinthians 12:26)

REFLECT AND RESPOND

Journaling Questions

> How do you feel when someone isn't listening to you? What about the opposite—when you can really tell you're being heard?

> How does showing empathy help others feel like they belong?

> What's one way you can practice empathy this week?

Pray This Prayer

God, you are the ultimate best listener. You always hear us when we're happy, sad, frustrated, or confused. Help me to be a good listener and to show empathy to my friends and family. I want to create a safe space of belonging. In Jesus' name, amen.

SOMETHING TO TRY

Read about a current event in the news and think about how the people in the story might be feeling. Write down how you would feel, and try to see the situation from various points of view. After you've thought about it on your own, bring someone else into your thought process and ask them how they would feel. Having this conversation will help you see how a situation can be experienced in multiple ways, building your empathy for others.

THE TAKEAWAY

Empathy starts with listening and grows into belonging.

POST 32

People-Pleasing ≠ Belonging

Are you a people pleaser?

Welcome to the club. We all struggle with people-pleasing to a certain degree—some more than others—but it's a pretty common experience.

People-pleasing can seem like a good idea in the moment, but it rarely ends well. Eventually, it gets impossible to please everyone, and you'll end up burned out and resentful. People-pleasing can feel like juggling; ultimately, the balls will drop, and you'll be disappointed in yourself.

If you've fallen into patterns of people-pleasing in some of your relationships, chances are you were looking for belonging. There was a person you wanted to be friends with, a teacher whose approval you were seeking, or a group you desperately wanted to be accepted into.

Wanting to belong in and of itself is not a bad thing. We were created to belong. It's normal. The problem is when we think certain unhealthy tactics will gain us that belonging. People-pleasing is one of those unhealthy tactics.

The Truth about People-Pleasing

We think that if we please the person whose relationship we're seeking, they will like and accept us. That may be true for a short while, but how long can we be expected to keep that up? It's likely that we will end up giving in and never speaking up for our own desires. That type of friendship is unbalanced and can get toxic.

Healthy relationships require boundaries, give-and-take, with everyone feeling safe enough to state their truth.

The apostle Paul knew the dangers of people-pleasing all too well. In chapter 1 of his letter to the church in Galatia (vv. 6–10), he called them out for following a gospel other than the one he preached. The Galatians knew the truth but didn't know how to stand up for it. They allowed false teachers to come into their community and spread lies.

Paul was outraged! Because of people-pleasing, the church was being deceived. Jesus was being misrepresented—a serious wrongdoing. Paul let them know that people-pleasing was unsuitable for a Christian because the only person we are accountable to is Jesus.

And you know what? You already have his approval.

While people-pleasing may gain you someone's approval for a short while, it won't last. You will have to keep performing.

God, on the other hand, has already approved of you because of who you are in Christ. Nothing you do or don't do can ever change that.

You can leave people-pleasing behind, because what you're seeking is already yours.

READING GOD'S WORD

Am I now trying to win the approval of human beings, or of God? Or am I trying to please people? If I were still trying to please people, I would not be a servant of Christ. (Galatians 1:10 NIV)

People are trapped by their fear of others;
those who trust the Lord are secure. (Proverbs 29:25)

We have been examined and approved by God to be trusted with the good news, and that's exactly how we speak. We aren't trying to please people, but we are trying to please God, who continues to examine our hearts. (1 Thessalonians 2:4)

REFLECT AND RESPOND

Journaling Questions

Do you struggle with people-pleasing? Why do you think that is?

Have you ever felt the negative effects of people-pleasing? What were they?

Does knowing you already have the approval and acceptance of God change anything for you? In what ways?

Pray This Prayer

God, I am so thankful that you already approve of me and love me. I never have to work to gain your love, because it's already mine. Next time I feel the temptation to people-please, remind me that I don't have to do that. May I walk in the truth of who I am in Christ. In Jesus' name, amen.

SOMETHING TO TRY

Sometimes the hardest thing to do to combat people-pleasing is saying no. If you have a hard time saying no to people's requests, this is a great exercise to try!

Get together with a trusted friend and practice saying no. This may feel awkward, but the more you get used to saying no out loud, the easier it will be when you're in a real situation in which you want to draw a boundary.

Make up scenarios that usually make you uncomfortable, and practice saying no to each other.

Want to go to the movies? *No, thanks!*

Will you share your math notes with me? *No, that's not a good idea.*

Let's skip class tomorrow. *No, I'd rather not.*

Some scenarios in which you might want or need to say no include:

- When you feel taken advantage of
- When it's not your problem
- When you just don't feel like doing something
- When you would rather do something else
- When it doesn't align with your values or beliefs

THE TAKEAWAY

We may think people-pleasing is the price we must pay for acceptance, but it's not worth it because we are already fully accepted by God.

POST 33

When You Are Dating

Dating is complicated at any age, but it can be especially confusing as a teenager.

What's the point of dating? Is it a precursor to marriage? Is it just for fun? How do you set boundaries? Should you have your parents' approval to date? Should the person you date share your beliefs? Why do so many people get hurt in dating relationships? Where is the teenage-dating manual?!

Yeah, that doesn't exist. Sorry.

Dating is going to look different depending on a lot of factors such as age, level of maturity, family dynamics, and cultural expectations. But here's the key: *healthy dating is based on respect.* Respect for yourself, your partner, and your family's rules.

We asked one sixteen-year-old what she had learned about herself in a high school dating relationship, and she shared, "I learned I have to be more self-confident. . . . A lot of times, if you say no to something, the person you're dating kind of makes you feel bad about it. So you do it anyway. I wish I had been more confident so I could have stuck with my no instead of giving in."

R-E-S-P-E-C-T

The truth of the matter is no one should ever feel pressured to do anything they don't want to do in a dating relationship. When we have respect for one another, we won't pressure, belittle, or act carelessly with our feelings or bodies.

Dating doesn't have to be taboo. It is good and normal to want to explore relationships, and dating is a great way to get to know someone. You'll experience big feelings that may be confusing, and that's okay too.

More than likely, heartbreak will occur.

More than likely, you'll shed tears over a breakup.

More than likely, emotions like jealousy or doubt will arise.

These experiences are all part of learning what kinds of relationships work for you. Exploring compatibility and what's important to you in a relationship takes time and experience.

The more you mature, the more you realize that being in a dating relationship is an honor and privilege. Having access to someone's heart is precious. The heart can be fragile and must be handled with care—yours included! It's important to enter into any relationship with your eyes wide open and a commitment to care for and respect yourself and the person you're dating.

The Bible invites us to "be the best at showing honor to each other" (Romans 12:10). While this passage isn't specifically about dating, this is the general attitude we should have toward anyone we encounter. When we lead with honor, we will act with integrity, decency, honesty, righteousness, and virtue. And we will expect others to treat us with that same respect. We don't need to tolerate anything less.

God loves you and wants the best for you. God doesn't want you to be stuck in a relationship in which you are not loved, respected, or cared for. Just as the heart of the person you're dating is precious, so is yours. Care for your own heart first, and expect nothing less in return.

READING GOD'S WORD

Love should be shown without pretending. Hate evil, and hold on to what is good. Love each other like the members of your family. Be the best at showing honor to each other. (Romans 12:9–10)

Those who pursue righteousness and kindness
will find life, righteousness, and honor. (Proverbs 21:21)

REFLECT AND RESPOND

Journaling Questions

What have your experiences with dating been like so far?

What are some of the expectations or views around dating in your family, your church, and your school? What are some of your own expectations for dating? How do these expectations differ from one another?

Why is respect so important in a relationship?

Pray This Prayer

God, you care for and love me so much. As your child, I know you want what's best for me and that includes what's best in my dating life. Help me to be honorable in my relationships. Help me to maintain boundaries in which I feel safe, respected, and loved. In Jesus' name, amen.

SOMETHING TO TRY

Ask a trusted adult if you can have a conversation about dating. This can be a parent, guardian, aunt, uncle, or youth worker from your church. In your conversation, ask them about their dating life when they were a teenager and what they learned from their experiences. You can also share with them any questions or experiences you may be struggling with.

THE TAKEAWAY

Take care of your own heart and your partner's by treating one another with respect.

POST 34

How to Get the Mentoring You Need

Wouldn't it be great to have the kind of mentoring and coaching Luke Skywalker had in the original *Star Wars* trilogy?

First, he had Obi-Wan Kenobi. Obi-Wan was instrumental in Luke's early lightsaber training. He single-handedly freed Luke and his companions from certain death by sacrificing himself to Darth Vader. That's quite a mentor! Unfortunately, with Obi-Wan's final, heroic act, he left Luke on his own to fight for truth, justice, and the Jedi way.

But then Luke ended up with Yoda as a mentor. One downside to Yoda's mentoring was that Luke had to carry him around on his back (but at least that made him portable).

Yoda was constantly whispering all sorts of pithy phrases in Luke's ear. Granted, most of them were over Luke's head. But still, Luke was trained day and night by a wise Jedi master whose nine hundred years of experience were unmatched in the galaxy.

Though it's often the case in movies, the type of mentoring Luke received from Obi-Wan and Yoda is not very likely to happen to us. Obi-Wan and Yoda were with Luke 24/7. They helped him with everything from lifting starfighters out of swamps to challenges of the will and body.

These days few people can give that kind of time or have that kind of power.

A Constellation of Mentors

As we face big and small questions where we could use some wise advice, it's often hard to find such be-all, end-all mentors. It's easy to give up on finding a wise coach when no Yoda drifts into our lives and promises to make us a better person, he will.

Years ago, I (Kara) took a class on leadership that changed my view of mentoring, especially in those times when there aren't enough mentors to go around.

Instead of expecting one perfect, all-encompassing mentor, what if we had a constellation of mentors—a small galaxy perhaps? No single mentor will be perfect, but each can speak into our lives, and they all can provide us with the diverse community of belonging we need.

Here's more good news from research: as you grow closer to Christ-centered adults, your relationship with Jesus can become stronger and more vibrant. In other words, while it's great to spend time with people your own age, being connected to trustworthy adults (in what we call "intergenerational relationships") can help you develop a faith that lasts.

READING GOD'S WORD

> Plans fail for lack of counsel,
> but with many advisers they succeed. (Proverbs 15:22 NIV)

REFLECT AND RESPOND

Journaling Questions

> What decisions are you facing, what plans are you trying to make, or what questions are you wrestling with?

Whom do you know who is older and trustworthy and might have some wise advice?

How do you think connecting with them might help in what you're wrestling with and also in your faith?

Pray This Prayer

God, thank you that you have designed us to walk through life in community instead of walking alone. Please help me to know the right mentors to talk to at the right times to get the advice I need. When I feel intimidated or nervous about reaching out, may your grace give me strength and courage. If there is a potential mentor I need to reach out to right now, please make that clear to me. In Jesus' name, amen.

SOMETHING TO TRY

Sometimes our attempts at finding mentors get stalled because we don't know how to ask someone older for help. If you're struggling with asking, try this script this week: "I'm realizing I could use some advice as I try to figure out [fill in the blank with your top questions]. I think maybe you could help me. Could we please have a short conversation about this sometime?"

Our experience is that when a teenager like you asks for a conversation about a specific topic, almost all adults will say, "Sure." Often that single discussion is an on-ramp to multiple conversations and a longer-term coaching relationship.

THE TAKEAWAY

Never face your tough life questions alone; instead, ask one or more adults for the help you need.

POST 35

Being a True Neighbor

> We settle for the illusion of separation when we are endlessly asked to enter into kinship with all.
>
> Gregory Boyle[1]

At the start of this book, we said that Jesus was asked hundreds of questions. Sometimes in response to those questions, Jesus would tell a story.

Once, when asked about how to get eternal life, Jesus answered, "'Love the Lord your God with all your heart and with all your soul and with all your strength and with all your mind'; and, 'Love your neighbor as yourself'" (Luke 10:27 NIV). Caught off guard, the legal expert who questioned Jesus shot back, "And who is my neighbor?" (v. 29 NIV).

The way Jesus responded to this seemingly simple question was with a profound and meaningful story. You may have heard of this story before. It's commonly known as "The Good Samaritan" (vv. 25–37), but this designation has its roots in deep prejudice. We could also call it "The True Neighbor."

To fully appreciate the story of this Samaritan neighbor, it's necessary to understand the history between Jews and Samaritans. Simply put, they were enemies. While both groups had a shared faith history, somewhere along the way they had veered away from one another.

Jews looked down on Samaritans for being of mixed ethnicity: half-Jew and half-Gentile. Most Jews avoided Samaria at all costs and wouldn't travel through there. They had political and cultural differences that seemed insurmountable to them, so they tried hard to ignore one another.

So you can imagine the surprise on the legal expert's face when Jesus tells a story in which a Samaritan is the hero! A priest and a Levite, men of honor in the Jewish community, each passed by a Jewish man who had been beaten and robbed. Only the hated Samaritan stopped to help the man—going so far as to pay two days' wages to ensure the man would be cared for.

The legal expert was forced to admit that the Samaritan was indeed good—that he had been a true neighbor to the man who was robbed.

Why Is This Important?

Jesus illustrates a point here—that everyone you meet is your neighbor. This means we all belong to one another. It doesn't matter what labels the world may try to pin on someone; they are still your neighbor. It doesn't matter what part of the city they live in, the type of music they listen to, or whether they like science or sports or comic books.

Every person you come in contact with is your neighbor, worthy of love, respect, and care.

Pastor Miles McPherson has said, "You should never put a label on anyone because you can't love people above the label you give them. That's why the only label you should give someone is 'neighbor.'"[2]

READING GOD'S WORD

> "Which of these three do you think was a neighbor to the man who fell into the hands of robbers?"
>
> The expert in the law replied, "The one who had mercy on him."
>
> Jesus told him, "Go and do likewise." (Luke 10:36–37 NIV)

All the Law has been fulfilled in a single statement: *Love your neighbor as yourself.* (Galatians 5:14)

REFLECT AND RESPOND

Journaling Questions

What does it mean to be a true neighbor to someone?

Who is someone you might not think of as your neighbor? How, if at all, does the story of the true neighbor change your perspective?

Pray This Prayer

God, you are good to give us neighbors and the opportunity to be neighbors to others. Just as the Samaritan neighbor in Jesus' story sacrificially loved and cared for the Jewish man who was robbed, help me to do likewise. Remind me even in the most difficult circumstances that we belong to each other. In Jesus' name, amen.

SOMETHING TO TRY

Make a list of five people who are your "neighbors."

Next to their names write a way you can show them love.

Pray about an opportunity that is personalized and meaningful to each individual. Pay attention to their needs, and think about something that will make a significant impact.

THE TAKEAWAY

Everyone you meet, no matter who they are or where they come from, is your neighbor.

POST 36

Finding Unity While Keeping Diversity

> At our church, we call each other by "brother" or "sister" because we are all brothers and sisters in Christ—because God made us all equal. We treat each other like family. That's how the church should be, being a whole family in Christ. We're very connected.
>
> Daniel

I (Kristel) grew up in Miami, Florida. Something I love about Miami is the diversity. If you have a craving for any specific cuisine, chances are you'll be able to find just the right restaurant to satisfy your appetite. I have friends who immigrated to Miami from all over the world. Getting to know them and their cultures was always fun and interesting. But if I'm honest, there were also divisions among cultures all over the city.

There were neighborhoods and communities for all the various ethnic groups. The Cubans stayed in Little Havana and the Haitians in Little Haiti. Doral was for Venezuelans and Sweetwater for Nicaraguans. Overtown had a majority Black population, while Miami Beach had a majority Jewish population. Each neighborhood and people group had a reputation, and some groups simply wouldn't mix.

A New Ethnic Identity

Miami is reminiscent of the ancient city of Antioch, one of the largest and most diverse cities in the known world. Antioch was divided by walls, and ethnic tensions were high. People didn't want to mix.

In the first century, your ethnicity was determined by your culture and religious background. Jews and Gentiles especially didn't have dealings with each other. But that all changed in Antioch.

When the church was getting started, mostly Jews were coming to faith in Jesus. Some followers of Jesus began to share the good news with Gentiles in this city, and they believed. Suddenly, these two groups started coming together, so much so that a new identity was born. Antioch is where believers were first called *Christians*, because they were a new group made up of both Jews and Gentiles. This was a significant cultural breakthrough.

The Christians in Antioch demonstrated unity within diversity. While they came from varying backgrounds, they were able to maintain unity through learning to follow Jesus. That's because unity does not mean uniformity. God does not require us all to be the same, but he does require us all to treat one another with equal value.

We can preserve who we are and come together in our differences. It makes for a more beautiful, interesting, diverse church.

READING GOD'S WORD

> Here there is no Gentile or Jew, circumcised or uncircumcised, barbarian, Scythian, slave or free, but Christ is all, and is in all. (Colossians 3:11 NIV)

> The Lord's power was with them, and a large number came to believe and turned to the Lord.
>
> When the church in Jerusalem heard about this, they sent Barnabas to Antioch. When he arrived and saw evidence of God's grace, he was overjoyed and encouraged everyone to remain fully committed to the Lord. Barnabas responded in this way because he was a good man,

whom the Holy Spirit had endowed with exceptional faith. A considerable number of people were added to the Lord. Barnabas went to Tarsus in search of Saul. When he found him, he brought him to Antioch. They were there for a whole year, meeting with the church and teaching large numbers of people. It was in Antioch where the disciples were first labeled "Christians." (Acts 11:21–26)

REFLECT AND RESPOND

Journaling Questions

What is difficult about maintaining unity within diversity?

Do you have a diverse friend group? If so, what do you love about it? If not, how can you pursue diversity in your friendships?

Pray This Prayer

God, thank you for the beautifully diverse way you created us. Help us all to see the beauty in diversity, and help us to pursue unity within our diversity. We know it is possible because you made a way through Jesus. Thank you. In Jesus' name, amen.

SOMETHING TO TRY

Get a clean piece of paper and draw twelve circles all the same size—four rows of three circles each. Starting with these circles that are all the same, draw something different with each one. Faces, animals, emojis, machines—it's up to your imagination. Look at how much diversity you can create from one starting shape! This is diversity within unity.

THE TAKEAWAY

Unity does not mean uniformity. We can all be different and still belong.

POST 37

Belonging in a Digital World

Like most of his peers, twelfth grader Michael spends a few hours a day on Instagram, Snapchat, TikTok, and text messaging. But he worries about the downside of technology: "I feel like our security is in technology. You don't want to talk to people, so you just text them or something like that. I just feel like we have lost a sense of having a real relationship with people around us and having face-to-face conversations."

Another teenager, Arthur, describes the complicated advantages and disadvantages of technology: "Social media and texting help me talk with my friends and get closer to them. But social media also helps people badmouth others, which people have done to me. So I cut off my social contact with those people. So yeah, for me, it goes both ways. I agree that it can do good, but it can potentially also do bad."

When social media is used for enhancing relationships, it can become a useful tool for reducing loneliness. Staying in touch with friends through social media can increase our connections.

But the opposite also happens. When social media is used as an escape from interacting in person with others, we lose out. It can become easy to "hide in plain sight" on devices to protect ourselves from rejection, but hiding comes at the cost of increasing loneliness.

Social media, like most things in life, has the power of good and evil. While there may be pitfalls in the digital world, there can also be great opportunities for connection.

Navigating Our Digital World

Each of us can think through how we want to interact on social media, gaming, and other virtual spaces. Setting boundaries and establishing ground rules before logging in can be helpful. Here are some ideas:

- Ask yourself why you're showing up in these spaces.
- Notice how you feel after spending time on social media or gaming.
- Set up boundaries for whom you will follow or interact with online.

Instead of engaging with the virtual world carelessly, take the time to truly understand what you're looking for.

While the Bible may not speak directly to social media and the internet, it has plenty to say about how we interact with one another and the impact of what we consume. We can foster belonging and true connection wherever and however we're with others.

READING GOD'S WORD

> Therefore, as God's choice, holy and loved, put on compassion, kindness, humility, gentleness, and patience. Be tolerant with each other and, if someone has a complaint against anyone, forgive each other. As the Lord forgave you, so also forgive each other. And over all these things put on love, which is the perfect bond of unity. The peace of Christ must control your hearts—a peace into which you were called in one body. And be thankful people. The word of Christ must live in you richly. Teach and warn each other with all wisdom by singing psalms, hymns, and spiritual songs. Sing to God with gratitude in your

hearts. Whatever you do, whether in speech or action, do it all in the name of the Lord Jesus and give thanks to God the Father through him. (Colossians 3:12–17)

REFLECT AND RESPOND

Journaling Questions

What are your favorite and least favorite social things to do on digital devices? What do you get out of that time?

Have you been able to make new or deeper connections in the digital world? What is special about those connections?

What's one way you can be wise in navigating the online world?

Pray This Prayer

God, thank you for the many ways you help us find connections in our world. Help me to be wise in the ways I interact online, and help me to use social media for good. In Jesus' name, amen.

SOMETHING TO TRY

Take an audit of your online life by asking: How much time do I spend on which devices, platforms, and games? What do I do online? Whom do I connect with? How do I feel when I log off?

Once you complete your review, write down a few guidelines you'd like to set for how and with whom you will interact in the digital world.

THE TAKEAWAY

The digital world can be a great space for connection, but it can also be complicated and painful. Think wisely about how you want to show up in virtual spaces.

POST 38

Lamenting Our Losses Together

Life isn't always butterflies and rainbows. Um, 2020 and beyond, anyone?

If we've learned anything through this pandemic, it's that life can be painful and disorienting. Doubt, fear, anger, disappointment, and grief are all emotions that are part of being human.

Sometimes it's tempting to try to hold those feelings from one another—and from God. We might feel like we'll be judged or even rejected. But the Bible is filled with stories, poems, and songs written by and about people who were sometimes very disappointed, and who brought those disappointments to God.

Room for All Our Feelings

Scripture calls this type of honest prayer *lament*.[1]

In lament we pour out our emotions to God—pain, doubt, grief—and then remind ourselves and one another that God is still with us. Lament doesn't always finish with a happy ending. Sometimes heartache comes and stays for a long time, but God is still there.

Maybe I (Brad) am kind of a downer, but laments are some of my favorite psalms. I like the raw, uncomfortable edges, the full breadth of human experience. Think about your favorite sad song—maybe about a breakup or bad relationship. Sometimes you feel better after you play a song like that, right? That's the power of lament.

The point of lament isn't to make everything better; the point is to make room for all our feelings. God isn't only interested in our cheerful, grateful attitudes but also welcomes us in our disappointment, frustration, rage, and devastation. Even when we feel those emotions toward God. I don't know about you, but that's comforting for me to know.

Today we're going to read a psalm of lament. You might want to prepare yourself first by closing your eyes for a minute and taking a few deep breaths.

When you're ready, slowly read through the psalm printed in the "Reading God's Word" section or read it in your own Bible. The writer of Psalm 77 has basically created two lists. The first ten verses line up complaints against God without holding much back. Then in verse 11, the list switches to the character and actions of God. This is how we lament.

Read through the passage a couple of times, paying attention to the emotions it brings up in you.

READING GOD'S WORD

I cry out loud to God—
  out loud to God so that he can hear me!
During the day when I'm in trouble I look for my Lord.
  At night my hands are still outstretched and don't grow
    numb;
  my whole being refuses to be comforted.
I remember God and I moan.
  I complain, and my spirit grows tired. *Selah*

You've kept my eyelids from closing.
  I'm so upset I can't even speak.
I think about days long past;
  I remember years that seem an eternity in the past.

I meditate with my heart at night;
  I complain, and my spirit keeps searching:
"Will my Lord reject me forever?
  Will he never be pleased again?
Has his faithful love come to a complete end?
  Is his promise over for future generations?
Has God forgotten how to be gracious?
  Has he angrily stopped up his compassion?" *Selah*
It's my misfortune, I thought,
  that the strong hand of the Most High is different now.

But I will remember the LORD's deeds;
  yes, I will remember your wondrous acts from times long past.
I will meditate on all your works;
  I will ponder your deeds.
God, your way is holiness!
  Who is as great a god as you, God?
You are the God who works wonders;
  you have demonstrated your strength among all peoples.
With your mighty arm you redeemed your people;
  redeemed the children of Jacob and Joseph. *Selah* (Psalm 77:1–15)

REFLECT AND RESPOND

Journaling Questions

Is it comfortable or uncomfortable for you to pray words like this writer prayed to God? Why?

> Verses 11–15 of Psalm 77 focus on who God is and gratitude for God's great actions. In the midst of times when you lament to God, what do you want to remember about God?

> How do you lament with others? What could it look like to be more candid with your less-than-happy feelings around some other Christians?

Pray This Prayer

God who is with me in both joy and sorrow, remind me today that it's safe to be honest with you about whatever I'm feeling. Give me safe people in my life who can accept me and all my uncomfortable emotions. In Jesus' name, amen.

SOMETHING TO TRY

Create your own two lists. First, write down your doubts, hurts, fears, and disappointments. Take courage from the author of Psalm 77, and don't hold anything back.

Then write another list of what you know to be true about God. Think through the character and actions you've heard about God from the Bible, but also think through your own life. Where has God been present and faithful to you?

Pray that God will see and hear all the things on your first list, and that God will be with you as you lean into trusting the second list to be true. Consider sharing your lists with someone you trust and lamenting together.

THE TAKEAWAY

We belong to God as our full selves, without needing to hide any of our emotions.

POST 39

Celebrating with Others

Celebration is a funny thing. It sounds cool and exciting. Who doesn't love a good party?! But it can get complicated when you feel like you're missing out or overlooked in some way.

When the movie *Encanto* came out, I (Kristel) was excited to see it! My husband is Colombian, and seeing Colombia represented on the big screen was a huge deal for our family. I immediately fell in love with the movie. The songs, the colors, the Latino vibrancy. I cried tears of joy.

Then *Encanto* was available for streaming and my daughter insisted we watch it every single day. I thought I would soon tire of it, but instead I gained new insights with each viewing. I won't give too much away, but the plot of the movie is about a "fantastical and magical" family.[1] Each member has a gift—Luisa is super strong, Camilo can shape-shift, Isabela can make flowers grow in an instant, Julieta can heal anyone with her delicious arepas—and they are all expected to use their gifts to help their village.

But Mirabel, the main character, has no gift. For reasons unknown, she was never given one, and she has had to live with that unmet desire. She is still holding out for a miracle that someday she can be special like everyone else in her family.

One day, after watching the movie for probably the fifth time, my daughter told me, "I think I know what Mirabel's gift is. She loves her family."

And you know what? She's right!

Celebration Is Love

Mirabel, despite having no obvious magical gift of her own, is steadfast in loving her *familia*. Right at the start of the movie, she sings all about her amazing family and celebrates their gifts. Her joy is palpable and compelling.

And when it's time for her little cousin Antonio to have his gift ceremony, she is with him every step of the way. Although she feels the pain of being the only one without a gift, she is supportive of Antonio and celebrates with him when he receives his magical gift of being able to communicate with animals.

I won't give the ending away, but know that the celebration is returned and it's worth the watch.

As members of God's family, we are also called on to celebrate one another. There's simply no room for jealousy, competition, or rivalry. We celebrate one another because we all belong to the same family and our gifts are meant to be shared to build each other up.

READING GOD'S WORD

> Continue encouraging each other and building each other up, just like you are doing already. (1 Thessalonians 5:11)

> Let us consider each other carefully for the purpose of sparking love and good deeds. Don't stop meeting together with other believers, which some people have gotten into the habit of doing. Instead, encourage each other, especially as you see the day drawing near. (Hebrews 10:24–25)

REFLECT AND RESPOND

Journaling Questions

When was the last time you celebrated someone else? Reflect on that experience.

How do you feel when people celebrate you?

How can you be better at celebrating others, even when it's difficult for you?

Pray This Prayer

God, what a joy it is that we get to celebrate one another! May I never forget my calling to celebrate and encourage my fellow brothers and sisters in Christ. In Jesus' name, amen.

SOMETHING TO TRY

Find a way to celebrate someone in your life this week. Here are some ideas:

- Make a colorful card for someone celebrating them! It can be for a big occasion, like a birthday or graduation, or a small victory, like finishing a school project or a sports season.

- Give someone a shout-out on social media! Be specific in your celebration. Share about a trait, characteristic, or talent you admire about them.
- Treat someone to coffee or dessert in celebration of an accomplishment they've been working toward, even if they haven't achieved it yet! We can celebrate the journey as much as the destination.

THE TAKEAWAY

Celebrating others is one way we can show love, especially as members of God's *familia*.

Connecting with God's Presence Anytime

Did you know that most of us don't breathe properly?[1]

We tend to breathe shallowly and rapidly through our chest and shoulders, which doesn't provide the ideal amount of oxygen to our brain and body. Instead, the best breathing uses the diaphragm (so that your abdomen moves out as you inhale and in as you exhale) at a rate of about six to eight breaths per minute.

Try breathing like this for a few minutes:

1. Find a quiet place to sit up straight with your feet flat on the floor.
2. Notice your breathing. What does it feel like to take air into your lungs? What does it feel like to exhale?
3. Now focus on breathing with your diaphragm (place your hand on your abdomen—it should be moving in and out).
4. Slow down your breaths, taking about five seconds to inhale and about the same to exhale.

Breathing to Belong

How did it feel to breathe with your diaphragm?

Think about this: each breath you've taken today—and every other breath you have ever taken—is a gift from God. One of God's first acts of love toward us is to give us life and breath.

Genesis 2:7 tells a story about God creating the first human and breathing life into his nostrils. Not only would humanity carry God's image into the new world, but we would also bear God's breath in our lungs.

That means God is as close as our breath. So maybe all we need to do to remember that God is with us is to stop and take a deep breath. Breathing is a sign of belonging—a reminder that God is near.

Someday we'll take our last breath, and none of us know when that day will be. In between, whenever we breathe in and out, we're experiencing God's presence in a small way.

READING GOD'S WORD

> The LORD God formed the human from the topsoil of the fertile land and blew life's breath into his nostrils. The human came to life. (Genesis 2:7)

> Naked I came from my mother's womb, and naked shall I return there; the LORD gave, and the LORD has taken away; blessed be the name of the LORD. (Job 1:21 NRSV)

REFLECT AND RESPOND

Journaling Questions

> When do you think you do your best breathing? When is it hardest to breathe well?

Is it easy or tough to sense God's presence when you focus on just breathing? Why do you think that is?

What does having the presence of God with you mean to you?

Pray This Prayer

Creator God, thank you for making me and giving me your own breath to show that I belong with you. Remind me of this belonging and of your presence as I breathe in and out today. In Jesus' name, amen.

SOMETHING TO TRY

Christians have used "breath prayers" through the centuries, combining breathing and praying (pretty obvious, right?). The idea is to say the first phrase of the prayer breathing in, the next phrase breathing out, and so on. One of the most common breath prayers is called the "Jesus prayer," which is sometimes shortened like the second or third lines:

Lord Jesus Christ, Son of God, have mercy on me, a sinner.
Lord Jesus, have mercy on me.
Lord, have mercy.

Try saying this prayer as you breathe in and out, at home or on the go.

THE TAKEAWAY

God's own breath is in your lungs. Breathing is a sign of belonging.

PART 3

WHAT DIFFERENCE CAN I MAKE?

The Big Question of PURPOSE

> I cannot answer the question, "What ought I to do?" unless I first answer the question, "Of which story am I a part?"
>
> Alasdair MacIntyre[1]

There's nothing quite like being drawn into a good story. A good story captivates us—transports us into another world, stirs up feelings, and leaves us inspired.

That's one of the reasons I (Kristel) have always loved reading and going to the movies. I love getting lost in good stories.

God also has a story—a greater story—and we're invited into it. That's why STORY is our key word for purpose.

God says our lives have meaning because we are part of a bigger story—the STORY of God and what God has done, is doing, and will do in the world. Our lives and the things we do matter, not because we perform for others' expectations, rules, or scripts but because our stories help advance the greater STORY of God through Jesus Christ.

Often throughout my life, I struggled with figuring out what I wanted *my* story to be. It seemed like I was surrounded by stories that wanted to claim my attention and direct my purpose.

Then I was introduced to God's STORY, and it changed how I viewed my purpose. My eyes were opened to the reality that God had given me a specific purpose related to my heritage, talents, and passions. The more I learned about God's STORY, the more God's purpose for my life was revealed.

As you read the posts in part 3, you will see that each of us finds our utmost meaning and purpose as a supporting character whose life revolves around God, Jesus, and the Holy Spirit, who are the authors and main characters.

In the words of the book of Hebrews, Jesus is the "author and perfecter of our faith" (12:2 ASV). Just as I'm learning more about God's STORY every day, I hope you grow in the daily joy of journeying with Jesus to discover your purpose.

POST 41

First Things First

How do I figure out what God wants me to do with my life?

How do I figure out what God wants me to do *today*?

These questions can feel overwhelming; sometimes you might even wish you had a script to follow or some kind of map to guide you forward. Or even that God would just speak directly and make it all clear!

One of the ways God speaks to us is through Scripture. While the Bible doesn't necessarily give us straightforward answers about our personal calling or decisions, Jesus does give an answer in Matthew 22 that clarifies our first calling: "*You must love the Lord your God with all your heart, with all your being, and with all your mind.* This is the first and greatest commandment. And the second is like it: *You must love your neighbor as you love yourself*" (vv. 37–39).

First things first, Jesus affirms that God's will for us is to love God with everything we are *and* to love our neighbor as ourself. This double "Great Commandment" is our ground rule—our starting point.

What Is Most Loving?

When we want to know what God wants us to do in a given situation, we can start by asking a simple question: *What is most loving?*

Loving God, others, and ourselves isn't always simple and surely isn't easy, but using love as a filter is a true guide.

In part 2 of this book, we looked at a story captured in Luke's Gospel (10:25–37) tied to this same commandment. The next question posed to Jesus was "Who is my neighbor?" (v. 29). In other words, *who am I responsible to love? Is it just the people who are like me, or people I don't like at all?*

Jesus answers with a story whose central character (a Samaritan) would have been scandalous to his listeners. What does this mean for us?

Showing mercy is an act of *being a neighbor* and *loving our neighbor*. It's also, by extension, a way to *love God*. And loving neighbors is not primarily about whether we're on the "right side" or believe the right things or worship the right way. It's not about being from a particular background or neighborhood. It's about seeing an opportunity to show love, mercy, kindness, or goodness to someone and choosing to say yes.

It's putting first things first.

When you put first things first, the rest will follow.

READING GOD'S WORD

"Teacher, what is the greatest commandment in the Law?"

He replied, "*You must love the Lord your God with all your heart, with all your being, and with all your mind.* This is the first and greatest commandment. And the second is like it: *You must love your neighbor as you love yourself.* All the Law and the Prophets depend on these two commands." (Matthew 22:36–40)

Love the LORD your God with all your heart, all your being, and all your strength. (Deuteronomy 6:5)

You must not take revenge nor hold a grudge against any of your people; instead, you must love your neighbor as yourself; I am the LORD. (Leviticus 19:18)

REFLECT AND RESPOND

Journaling Questions

> Does it make you more or less anxious to think about doing God's will through the lens of loving God and loving others? Why?

> Make three lists with the headings Love God, Love Others, Love Self. Under each heading, write ideas for how you can tangibly show love in each category. Include actions you're already taking, and brainstorm new ideas you could try. Go back and star something in each category you'll do this week.

Pray This Prayer

Lord, I want to follow you and to do your will. Open my eyes to see the people around me who need love, and give me the courage to act in love today. In Jesus' name, amen.

SOMETHING TO TRY

Set a daily alarm for about five minutes before you are supposed to walk out the door for school or begin school at home. If you're using a phone, call this alarm "First" or "First, love." When the alarm sounds each day, let it be a reminder that above all else, your call this day is first to love: love God, love others, and love yourself.

THE TAKEAWAY

Loving God and loving others are our first two calls. It's always the way to do God's will.

POST 42

Asking the Right Questions to Find Your Purpose

Questions are essential.

Asking the right questions is the key to *discovering* the right answers.

I'll admit, I (Kristel) talked so much and asked so many questions as a kid that it drove my parents crazy. They had to ask me to take breaks. Curiosity oozed out of me, and I wanted to know everything about everything.

At a young age, it's normal for our questions to seem disorganized or jumbled. As we grow and mature, however, it's important to think before we ask—to ask the right question with intentionality and an end in mind. It's important to take into consideration *whom* you're talking to, *where* the conversation is going, and *what* answers you're looking for.

Jesus was great at asking questions. In fact, most of the time when someone would ask *him* a question, he would respond with another question! Sometimes we want someone to tell us the answer so badly—but what we really need is to discover the answer for ourselves. It's when we ask ourselves the hard-but-meaningful questions that we will have our aha moment.

Jesus Asks Peter the Right Question

There's an exchange in the Bible between Jesus and Peter that I love to read. Let me give you the background.

At the Last Supper, Jesus is eating with his disciples and preparing to go to the cross. Jesus warns that he will be rejected, and that even his closest disciples will deny him. Peter is adamant that he will never deny Jesus. Peter loves Jesus too much to not tell the world. He has no shame, and he is not afraid.

But that all changes when Jesus is captured by the Roman soldiers. Mere hours after Peter pledges his full devotion, Peter is very much filled with fear. As he sits around the campfire with strangers talking about Jesus, a young girl says, "Hey, aren't you one of his friends?" Peter, caught off guard, denies this claim. In fact, he refuses to acknowledge that he is one of Jesus' followers two more times that night.

Peter then remembers the words of Jesus—that Peter too will deny him. Guilt washes over him, and he weeps.

Fast-forward to after Jesus rose from the dead. One of the times he appeared to the disciples was after they had been fishing. As Jesus and Peter sit on the beach eating fish around a fire, Jesus asks him, "Peter, do you love me?"

You can tell Peter is embarrassed by Jesus' question. He's ashamed and doesn't want to be reminded of the way he messed up. "Of course, I love you. You know that!"

"Take care of my sheep," Jesus responds. You see, Jesus is known as the Good Shepherd, and we are his sheep (John 10:1–18). He cares for us, protects us, and shelters us.

Again, Jesus asks Peter if Peter loves him. Again, Peter assures Jesus that he does. And again, Jesus calls on Peter to care for his sheep.

And then a third time, the same discussion occurs.

At this point, Peter is flabbergasted! It may seem like Jesus is badgering Peter, questioning his love, trying to test him. But that's not at all what's going on.

Instead, a beautiful reversal takes place. Three times Peter had denied Jesus around a fire, and three times Jesus gives Peter an opportunity to proclaim his love and commitment to Jesus around another fire.

It doesn't end there. Jesus shows Peter his purpose: *"Take care of my sheep."* Jesus knows he will be returning to God the Father. He wants Peter to know that it will now be his responsibility to care for those who remain on earth.

Jesus probably could have just told Peter his purpose without all the questions—but through the line of questioning, perhaps Peter realized he really did love Jesus and he really did want to be committed to Jesus' mission. And so, he knew what he had to do: take care of the people who follow Jesus.

READING GOD'S WORD

When they finished eating, Jesus asked Simon Peter, "Simon son of John, do you love me more than these?"

Simon replied, "Yes, Lord, you know I love you."

Jesus said to him, "Feed my lambs." Jesus asked a second time, "Simon son of John, do you love me?"

Simon replied, "Yes, Lord, you know I love you."

Jesus said to him, "Take care of my sheep." He asked a third time, "Simon son of John, do you love me?"

Peter was sad that Jesus asked him a third time, "Do you love me?" He replied, "Lord, you know everything; you know I love you."

Jesus said to him, "Feed my sheep." (John 21:15–17)

REFLECT AND RESPOND

Journaling Questions

What questions do you have about your purpose?

Do you think you're asking the right questions to get the right answers? What's one way you can discover if you're asking the right questions?

Whom can you discuss your questions with?

Pray This Prayer

God, thank you for your love and example in the Scriptures that you care about my purpose. As I begin to discover what that means for my life, help me to ask the right questions with a focus on what you want for my life. In Jesus' name, amen.

SOMETHING TO TRY

Make a list of the questions you have regarding your purpose. Sit down with a trusted adult to share your questions. Be open to the questions they ask you as you are challenged to think about God's purpose for your life.

THE TAKEAWAY

Jesus asked the right questions to help people discover their purpose. You can learn to ask the right questions too.

POST 43

No Purpose Is Better Than Another

> I think of myself like a pencil. I can try to be a utensil to eat with—like a fork or a chopstick—but that's not my purpose. Either I'm writing and being used for God's purposes or I'm not.
>
> Kevin

The quote at the start of this post from seventeen-year-old Kevin is profound in more ways than one.

First, he seems to have a solid understanding of what his particular purpose is. In his metaphor, he's a pencil. Pencils are useful and necessary. Pencils do great work. They write and draw and do all kinds of neat stuff.

But what if a pencil saw a fork and thought, "Huh, that fork gets used all the time. Look at how shiny it is. Everyone loves that fork. And the job that fork is doing looks really fun. I want to be a fork!" Imagine that pencil attempting to pick up rice or twist noodles around itself. That doesn't work—because it's a pencil, not a fork.

It may sound silly, but that's how we sound when we compare ourselves to others.

That's the second way Kevin's quote is profound. He sees that comparison is a waste of time because no purpose is greater than another.

A pencil and chopsticks are both great. They each serve a needed purpose. One can't say that a pencil is better than a chopstick or a chopstick is better than a pencil. When you're sitting down to eat dinner, you're going to want chopsticks, a fork, or a spoon. When you're sitting down to write a letter, you're going to want a pencil, a pen, or something else to write with. Not even the shiniest fork will help you then!

Stop Comparison

Do you ever get caught up in comparison? We all do. Sometimes we catch a glimpse of someone else's life, and it looks so shiny and fun. Social media feeds our insecurities as we get a front-row seat to everyone's highlight reel, not knowing that we may not get to see all the realities behind the scenes.

The fact of the matter is we all have different strengths. We have different gifts and passions. We are living in different seasons of life. These are all factors in our purpose and how we live out God's unique plan for us.

Instead of looking to the left and to the right, it's best to keep your eyes on *your* paper and focus on what God has called you to do.

Although we have different gifts, it's the same God who distributed them all. The Lord chose everyone's gifts on purpose and for a purpose. We can trust that God's intention is good and that we are not lacking in anything.

Think of your gift as your superpower. No one else has it but you, and it can serve a great purpose that changes the world. Iron Man had great intellect and tech capabilities. Captain America was strong and fast and honorable. The Hulk could transform into a giant beast. Thor was a legendary prince with a mystical hammer. Black Widow was a highly trained spy. Hawkeye was a master archer. They each possessed a superpower that was unique and indispensable—and when they joined forces as the Avengers, they saved the world—more than once!

When you and your superpower come together with others and their superpowers—that makes for an incredible team.

READING GOD'S WORD

There are different spiritual gifts but the same Spirit; and there are different ministries and the same Lord; and there are different activities but the same God who produces all of them in everyone. (1 Corinthians 12:4–6)

For we are God's handiwork, created in Christ Jesus to do good works, which God prepared in advance for us to do. (Ephesians 2:10 NIV)

REFLECT AND RESPOND

Journaling Questions

What's your superpower? What are you good at? What do you love to do?

What makes *your* gift special?

How can recognizing the uniqueness of your own gift help you stop comparing yourself to others?

Pray This Prayer

> *God, thank you for the amazing gift you have given me. When I start comparing myself to others, remind me that you gifted me in a specific way for a specific purpose. I don't have to wish I had someone else's gift or purpose. I have my own, and that's pretty special. In Jesus' name, amen.*

SOMETHING TO TRY

Sometimes it's helpful when we get an outside perspective. If you're having a hard time understanding what your gift is, get together with someone you trust and ask them what gift they see in you. You can then do the same for them!

THE TAKEAWAY

No purpose is greater than another. Your purpose is unique to your gift and passions—your own superpower!

POST 44

What If God Wants You to Make a Different Choice?

"Did you get the big envelope or the little envelope?"

This was a question high school seniors asked one another every spring when they heard from the colleges to which they had applied. There was no email, so all our communication with schools was by paper. If a school sent a little envelope, it was usually a single sheet of paper telling us we hadn't been admitted. If a school sent a big envelope, it meant we had been admitted and needed to complete a batch of paperwork.

As a senior, I (Kara) remember the Thursday I came home to check the mail after school. One of my closest friends had come with me because we had heard that my top choice school had mailed out its notices.

I opened the mailbox with trepidation.

It was the big envelope.

I remember ripping open the envelope to confirm it was a yes and then hugging my friend.

While that was a joyful afternoon, figuring out which school I would attend was not easy. The "big envelope" university was by far the most prestigious of my options—a "big deal" school. It made sense, and it was where my dad wanted me to go.

But my parents are divorced, and my mom wanted me to go to a different school.

A handful of church leaders I respected preferred a third school close to home that allowed me to stay involved in church even as a college student.

I couldn't make up my mind. I prayed a lot but couldn't tell where God was leading me. And the adults closest to me brought more confusion than clarity.

I struggled for over a month with what to do. But eventually, as I prayed more, I felt the most peace about going to the "big envelope" university. Not only did it make sense but it also felt like it was what God desired.

But I had gotten to the point that I was willing to go to the less big-deal school if it seemed like that was what God wanted.

Choosing God's Better Story

In one story in the Gospel of Luke, immediately after describing the suffering that awaits him in the future, Jesus gives a warning to his followers: "All who want to come after me must say no to themselves, take up their cross daily, and follow me" (9:23). Eventually, Jesus illustrated both this verse and the cost of discipleship by dying on a literal cross for all of us.

Sometimes being part of God's story seems easier. You and I get to make the choices most others would.

But sometimes being part of God's story means we say no when everyone else is saying yes. Following in the way of Jesus means we renounce other paths, allegiances, lords, and idols. We choose what's counterintuitive to others but makes sense as we think about God's story and the part God wants us to play in it.

Maybe you choose to help your mom and stepdad by babysitting your younger sister instead of going out with friends on Saturday afternoon.

Perhaps you make the choice to have lunch with the new kid at school instead of your close friends.

Or in my case, you ponder a less big-deal college or job because it feels like that may be what God wants. You're willing to toss aside the "big envelope" for the better story God has for you.

READING GOD'S WORD

Jesus said to everyone, "All who want to come after me must say no to themselves, take up their cross daily, and follow me." (Luke 9:23)

REFLECT AND RESPOND

Journaling Questions

As you approach decisions about your current and future purpose, how do you try to sense which path God wants you to take?

Whether it's big decisions about your future or smaller decisions about how you spend your time this afternoon, when have you felt it was right to go with the "big envelope" path—the one that made the most sense and seemed most logical?

> When have you felt led to not take the "big envelope" path because you felt like God had something better—and different—for you?

Pray This Prayer

God, some days I feel torn between doing what's easiest at the moment and doing what you most want me to do. When I hit those forks in the road, please help me to know what you want me to do. Then by your grace, please give me the strength and courage I need to make that choice—especially when it's difficult and different from what most everyone else would do. In Jesus' name, amen.

SOMETHING TO TRY

Focus on one decision you're trying to make right now. Reflect on different options you're considering. Ask God to give you the most peace about the path that God would want you to take. As you feel more peace about a certain path, continue to prayerfully hold that before the Lord. If it continues to feel right, then maybe that's the path you should take!

THE TAKEAWAY

Choosing God's path is sometimes hard, but it's always holy.

POST 45

God's Purpose for You Is Up to God

> I have a career in mind that I want to do, but I don't know if that's what God wants for me. What if I pursue it and it ends up not being God's best for me? I will have spent four years studying something only to scrap it and start all over. I keep changing my mind about what I want to be. I'm wondering how many times it will change before I finally land on what God wants me to do.
>
> Lilly

Lilly nervously admitted her anxiety about the future. As a person who wants to follow Jesus and live out God's purpose in her life, she wants to figure out "God's best" and "what God wants."

Do you ever worry about the future like Lilly? Like somehow God has a plan, but you have to figure it out, solve the mystery, put all the puzzle pieces together, or whatever metaphor you've heard about how this seems to work for other people?

That can be exhausting. I (Brad) remember feeling this exhaustion. I'm pretty sure I was asked at least once about my post–high school plans *every single day* of my senior year.

Maybe, like Lilly, you've had well-intentioned people in your life who teach about God's plan in a way that ends up stressing you out.

Lilly shared that her middle school pastor "really emphasized knowing God's vision for us. Ever since then, I've been tripped up about different paths I'm interested in, wondering which is God's vision for me. I have always been told that our purpose as humans is to advance God's kingdom, and I want to do that. But I'm stressed because I don't know how I'm supposed to do that."

Many of the teenagers we interviewed for our research felt the same pressure to have a clear sense about their future. One senior said he "feels like a failure" because "it feels like everyone else knows exactly what they're going to do. Not knowing makes you feel out of it and different."

God Has a Plan for That

If this post is raising your anxiety just by reading it, keep reading; we hope to take it down a notch or two. The thing is, God's plan isn't a game. And God's desire isn't to trick you or lead you the wrong way or shame you for choosing badly.

God's plan, purpose, vision, and future for you will unfold. You will be there, and God will be there. *With you.*

And maybe that's the most you need to know about God's plan. But here's something more from Scripture: *all things are held together in Jesus.*

This is an incredible plan! You aren't in charge here. You didn't exist before all things, you didn't create all things, and you don't hold all things together. God the Father, Son, and Holy Spirit have been at work since before time, and we can rest knowing Jesus holds everything together—so that job isn't up to us!

If God is holding *all things* together through Christ, that includes your future. It includes all the things you might be wondering about, like what to do after high school, what to do after that, whom you'll spend your life with, and where you'll go.

God's plan is to be *with* you, and Jesus will be holding *all things* together the entire way.

READING GOD'S WORD

The Son is the image of the invisible God,
the one who is first over all creation,

Because all things were created by him:
both in the heavens and on the earth,
the things that are visible and the things that are invisible.
Whether they are thrones or powers,
or rulers or authorities,
all things were created through him and for him.

He existed before all things,
and all things are held together in him. (Colossians 1:15–17)

REFLECT AND RESPOND

Journaling Questions

When you think about the future, what makes you most uneasy? What makes you most excited?

What are some of the ideas and phrases you've heard about God's plan or purpose for you? What's helpful or unhelpful about these messages?

How does it feel to know that Christ is at the center of all things, holding everything together—even your future?

Pray This Prayer

God, sometimes I worry that I might miss your plans for me or make a wrong decision that disappoints you. When I feel this way, remind me that you are always with me, and you are holding my life together, and let that be enough. In Jesus' name, amen.

SOMETHING TO TRY

Find a small paper bag somewhere around your home—one you can write on. Get a pen or marker and write out the words of Colossians 1:17 somewhere on the bag (or all over it!). On small pieces of scrap paper or Post-it notes, write some of the questions, fears, and hopes you have about your future, then fold each one and put it in the bag. As you drop each note in the bag, repeat Colossians 1:17 out loud.

Over the next week or so, add more until you feel as if you've captured enough. Then close the bag with tape or staples and either throw it out, tuck it away for later, or leave it where you can see it as a reminder that Jesus—not you—is holding it all together.

THE TAKEAWAY

God's not worried that you're going to mess up your future or somehow miss your purpose. Jesus will be with you, holding *all things* together the entire way.

POST 46

Putting Faith into Action

Anjezë (Agnes) Gonxhe was twelve years old when she made the decision to dedicate her life to serving God and people. Agnes grew up in the Catholic faith and had always been fascinated by the lives of missionaries. She knew she wanted to follow in their path.

At eighteen years old, she left home in Macedonia to study English with the goal of serving in India. Once she arrived in India, she began teaching at a school and took her vows as a nun. She chose to be named after Thérèse de Lisieux, the Catholic patron saint of missionaries. Eventually, she would be known as Mother Teresa.

You've probably heard of Mother Teresa—even jokingly (as in, "I'm no Mother Teresa!"). She gained notoriety for her selfless work serving among the poor and destitute of Calcutta, India. She refused to remain behind the walls of the convent teaching in the school; she wanted to be *with* the people beyond the walls who were suffering.

Love Is an Action

Mother Teresa once said, "Be kind and merciful. Let no one ever come to you without coming away better and happier."[1] Mother Teresa understood that her faith revolved around love, because love is an *action*. She didn't want to tell people she loved them or that God loved them—she wanted to *show* them.

And so, she did.

She started an open-air school for children who lived in slums and had no access to education. She provided food and health care to those who had none. She opened orphanages and hospices for those with leprosy and AIDS.

Was Mother Teresa perfect? Of course not! She struggled and had missteps throughout her life as we all do. No one, however, could question her dedication to her work among those in need in India. She knew her purpose and worked hard at it.

Mother Teresa once said we should not worry about doing big, impressive things but rather "do little things with great love" and "help one person at a time, and always start with the person nearest you."[2] We can heed these words in our own lives.

You don't have to go to India and start orphanages and health care centers. You can reach out to your elderly neighbor, the kid who sits next to you in math class, or your local homeless shelter—and show them love in a tangible way.

James, one of Jesus' younger brothers, knew that faith without action to back it up was meaningless. That's why in his letter to Christ followers, James challenges them to show evidence of their faith and love by meeting the needs of others. It does no good to pray for someone's needs if you're not willing to do something about them. That's how we put our faith into action.

READING GOD'S WORD

You must be doers of the word and not only hearers who mislead themselves. . . . True devotion, the kind that is pure and faultless before God the Father, is this: to care for orphans and widows in their difficulties and to keep the world from contaminating us. (James 1:22, 27)

If I speak in tongues of human beings and of angels but I don't have love, I'm a clanging gong or a clashing cymbal. (1 Corinthians 13:1)

REFLECT AND RESPOND

Journaling Questions

What stands out to you about Mother Teresa's work?

Why is it important to put our faith into action?

How is loving others a demonstration of your faith?

Pray This Prayer

God, you are a God of faith and a God of action. You chose to act first by sending your Son to rescue us from sin. As I learn to live out my faith, present me with opportunities to put my faith into action. Help me not to be overwhelmed by all the possibilities but help me to focus on helping the people around me. In Jesus' name, amen.

SOMETHING TO TRY

Reflect on the words of Mother Teresa: "Help one person at a time, and always start with the person nearest you."

Usually, the people nearest you live with you. Choose one person in your home and offer to help them in some way today.

THE TAKEAWAY

Authentic faith requires action, because love is a verb.

POST 47

Know God's Story so You Can Go in God's Story

There's a story told in Luke 24 about two friends walking from one town to the next. They recently had witnessed disturbing events. Their leader was executed—the leader they were counting on to bring lasting change to their people. As they walk together, their faces reflect the swirl of negative emotions inside—devastation, confusion, loss.

Suddenly, a man appears out of nowhere. He asks them what they're talking about, and they can't believe he doesn't know. Everyone either saw it with their own eyes or heard about it from those who were there. They begin to recount to him who their leader was and why he was handed over to a violent death.

But wait, there's more . . .

They also tell him that some women from their group saw angels who told them their leader is actually alive!

But there's no way that's true . . .

Plot Twist

They don't know it yet, but the stranger they're talking to is actually their leader. The women were right! He's alive! And he's right there with them.

He chooses not to reveal himself just yet, but what he does is maybe more valuable. He begins to tell them God's story from the beginning and how everything that has happened was foretold in the Scriptures. As he speaks, the puzzle pieces start to come together in their minds. They start to recognize God's story and how it all fits together.

Soon their eyes are opened, and they realize that the man they're talking to is Jesus.

They're overjoyed! But in an instant, he's gone.

Do you wonder why Jesus disappeared like that? Why he didn't stay to continue explaining or even just hang out? Perhaps he left because he knew they were ready. Now that they understood God's story, they were ready to *go in God's story*.

And that's exactly what they did. They got up and ran back to Jerusalem. They couldn't wait to tell the rest of the disciples all they had experienced. God's story was true—Jesus himself had enlightened them—this was all part of God's plan from the very beginning.

God's love for creation. God's purpose for creation. God's plan to rescue creation.

If you want to know and move forward in your purpose, it's necessary to know God's story first. It's all there. Being equipped with that understanding will help sustain you as you discover and live out your purpose. Instead of walking down the road feeling devastated, confused, and lost, you'll have your heart set on fire.

READING GOD'S WORD

They said to each other, "Weren't our hearts on fire when he spoke to us along the road and when he explained the scriptures for us?"

They got up right then and returned to Jerusalem. They found the eleven and their companions gathered together. They were saying to each other, "The Lord really has risen! He appeared to Simon!" Then the two disciples described what had happened along the road and how Jesus was made known to them as he broke the bread. . . .

Jesus said to them, "These are my words that I spoke to you while I was still with you—that everything written about me in the Law from Moses, the Prophets, and the Psalms must be fulfilled." Then he opened their minds to understand the scriptures. He said to them, "This is what is written: the Christ will suffer and rise from the dead on the third day, and a change of heart and life for the forgiveness of sins must be preached in his name to all nations, beginning from Jerusalem. You are witnesses of these things." (Luke 24:32–35, 44–48)

REFLECT AND RESPOND

Journaling Questions

What do you know about God's story?

How much would you say God is part of the way you see your story now? On a scale of 1 to 10 (with 1 being "not much" and 10 being "completely"), how much does your faith influence your story?

What would it take to encourage you to be ready to go in God's story?

Pray This Prayer

God, thank you for inviting me to know your story and to go in your story. You have an intentional purpose for my life. The more I know who you are and what your purpose is, the more I will be equipped to live out what I was created to do. Thank you for giving us what we need to live out your story. In Jesus' name, amen.

SOMETHING TO TRY

The story of Scripture can seem disjointed. Many people see the Old Testament and New Testament and assume they have little to do with each other. But the Bible is actually one big story—God's story. Jesus affirms this when he says that all Scripture testifies about who he is (v. 44). Jesus fulfills God's story.

Sometimes the big story of God is summarized in the Bible itself. Read the story of Stephen in Acts 6:8–8:2. Stephen was a disciple of Jesus who had a good grasp on the story of God. While he lost his life because he was bold enough to share this story, his death was not in vain. In fact, the message of Jesus began to spread beyond Jerusalem because of his death. Consider what stands out to you in Stephen's retelling of God's story.

THE TAKEAWAY

When you know God's story, you can go in God's story—and be better equipped to live out God's purpose for your life.

POST 48

What Is Discipleship?

Discipleship can be one of those "Christianese" words thrown around a lot in church circles, but what is it exactly?

At its core, discipleship is our *everyday yes to Jesus.*

It's been wisely said that when we follow Jesus, we say "one big yes" followed by a thousand little yeses each day. Discipleship is a journey, a long pilgrimage, grounded in the stuff of normal life. It's gritty, real, whole-person faith.

I (Kristel) was not unaware of faith when I was growing up, but I wouldn't say it was high on my priority list. I knew of Jesus and had learned some Bible stories but admittedly had never actually read the Bible. In high school, however, a friend invited me to her youth group, and I discovered new ways of being a disciple. Building on my early faith foundations, that season was really when I said yes to following Jesus. I was fascinated by viewing the world through the lens of faith, and I also discovered that there was a lot about the Bible I didn't know.

Our youth pastor, Mr. J, invited me to join a group of students every Tuesday afternoon to study the Bible and pray. It was there that I really began reading the Bible for the first time. This was the beginning of a new discipleship journey.

But it didn't end there. Mr. and Mrs. J also invited us over to their apartment on the weekends to hang out or play basketball in the church parking lot. When service opportunities came up, Mr. J would rally the teens and put us to work. On youth group nights, we learned about worshiping through music and through the preaching of the Bible. We also had fun playing foosball and eating pizza (which I discovered was the official food of youth groups).

Discipleship wasn't only going to worship or studying the Bible—it was also connecting with other Christ followers, serving others, and sharing meals. It reminds me of the early church we learn about in the book of Acts: "The believers devoted themselves to the apostles' teaching, to the community, to their shared meals, and to their prayers" (2:42).

What's Your Discipleship Journey?

The final words from Jesus to his disciples in the Gospel of Matthew are what many believers call "The Great Commission." He said, "Therefore, go and make disciples of all nations, baptizing them in the name of the Father and of the Son and of the Holy Spirit, teaching them to obey everything that I've commanded you" (28:19–20).

Jesus named three initial steps in the discipleship journey: (1) go, (2) make disciples, and (3) teach. As we read about the disciples in the early church, we see them follow these three steps as they share and serve one another.

So where are you in your discipleship journey? Have you said yes to Jesus? Are you in the process of learning and sharing the biblical story? Have you leaned into opportunities to serve and help others?

The thing to remember about this journey is that it isn't linear and that it looks different for everyone. There are first steps, but there is no formula for discipleship. It's our yes today to what God might put in front of us today.

Your next step may be baptism, while your friend's next step may be learning to pray. Your next step may be signing up to serve on a ministry team, while your friend's next step may be signing up for a Bible study.

Sometimes we take multiple steps at once. Sometimes they're giant steps. Sometimes they're baby steps. But you're not taking any of these steps on your own! We have been gifted the Holy Spirit, who walks in step with us and helps us in this journey. We've also been given each other—the church.

Most importantly, remember that this is a journey of love. That's who God is. God is love. And as we say yes to Jesus each day, we will grow in love.

In fact, that's what I remember most from those days in Mr. J's youth group. I remember how much he and his wife loved us. They cared about our lives. They cared about our good. They made house calls and listened to us and pointed us to our greater purpose. None of the rest of it would have mattered much without love.

READING GOD'S WORD

Jesus came near and spoke to them, "I've received all authority in heaven and on earth. Therefore, go and make disciples of all nations, baptizing them in the name of the Father and of the Son and of the Holy Spirit, teaching them to obey everything that I've commanded you. Look, I myself will be with you every day until the end of this present age." (Matthew 28:18–20)

As Jesus passed alongside the Galilee Sea, he saw two brothers, Simon and Andrew, throwing fishing nets into the sea, for they were fishermen. "Come, follow me," he said, "and I'll show you how to fish for people." Right away, they left their nets and followed him. (Mark 1:16–18)

I give you a new commandment: Love each other. Just as I have loved you, so you also must love each other. This is how everyone will know that you are my disciples, when you love each other. (John 13:34–35)

REFLECT AND RESPOND

Journaling Questions

> What has been your experience with discipleship? Is this a new word or concept for you?

> What do you think your next "everyday yes" to God might look like?

> How might discipleship help point you to your purpose?

Pray This Prayer

God, as I grow in my faith and go on this discipleship journey, I pray that I will grow in love. Thank you for the gift of your Spirit, who helps us to grow. Thank you for the gift of community, which helps us to grow. I pray that with each day that passes, I will say a new yes to Jesus. In Jesus' name, amen.

SOMETHING TO TRY

Seek out some time with a leader from your church. If you don't have a church, perhaps a parent or a friend can help you find one.

Sit down with this church leader to talk about how discipleship works at their church. Do they have a pathway for people to follow? Do they provide one-on-one mentorship? Take some time to explore what your next step could be.

THE TAKEAWAY

Discipleship is our ongoing faith journey of saying an *everyday yes* to Jesus.

POST 49

Our Steady Companion in an Unsteady World

Life is unpredictable. There are times when it feels like we're in the middle of a storm. Chaotic, messy, overwhelming—maybe even scary.

The disciples of Jesus knew something about storms. In fact, there was one storm in particular where they were so terrified and unsteady, they thought they might die! Gale-force winds? Waves crashing? Boat swamped? Yep, sounds like a regular Tuesday in our world too.

It's exhausting to go through life when everything is constantly changing and out of our control. The circumstances of life can feel so overwhelming that it's a wonder we get through them.

But there is one person in any storm who remains steady as a rock.

In the midst of this severe storm with his disciples, Jesus was in complete peace—in fact, he was so at peace, he decided to take a nap. *How could Jesus be asleep while everyone else on the boat was fearing for their lives?*

One of the names for Jesus in the Bible is the Prince of Peace. Sometimes we think peace means that everything is calm, quiet, and still. But peace is more than that. Jesus was peace in the middle of the storm—before he calmed the waves, he was already at peace.

The question Jesus asks the disciples is a signal to us. "Why are you frightened? Don't you have faith yet?" (Mark 4:40).

Did Jesus have peace because he had faith?

Faith and Peace

The link between faith and peace is profound—but the important part is what, or whom, you have faith in.

Jesus often talked about his Father—God. He would go away from his followers to spend time alone with God. In John 10:30, he says, "I and the Father are one." Their relationship was steady, and because of that, Jesus trusted that God was with Jesus and the disciples in the storm and would bring them through the storm.

We have access to the same peace Jesus carried because we have access to the same God Jesus had faith in. God is our steady companion in this unsteady world.

The story doesn't end there.

Jesus didn't just keep that peace for himself. When his followers were terrified, he got up and calmed the storm. The winds died down and the waves settled. He shared the peace.

You can do that too. Because once Jesus gives us peace, we don't keep it for ourselves. We're called to share that peace with others—it's part of our purpose.

READING GOD'S WORD

Later that day, when evening came, Jesus said to them, "Let's cross over to the other side of the lake." They left the crowd and took him in the boat just as he was. Other boats followed along.

Gale-force winds arose, and waves crashed against the boat so that the boat was swamped. But Jesus was in the rear of the boat, sleeping on a pillow. They woke him up and said, "Teacher, don't you care that we're drowning?"

He got up and gave orders to the wind, and he said to the lake, "Silence! Be still!" The wind settled down and there was a great calm. Jesus asked them, "Why are you frightened? Don't you have faith yet?"

Overcome with awe, they said to each other, "Who then is this? Even the wind and the sea obey him!" (Mark 4:35–41)

REFLECT AND RESPOND

Journaling Questions

Do you ever feel unsteady in this world? Why?

How can you find peace in Jesus when you feel unsteady?

Pray This Prayer

God, you are my peace in a world that often feels chaotic and out of control. You are my steady companion. Even when the waves are crashing and the winds are blowing—you are with me. Remind me of the peace that is already mine that I can have whenever I feel overwhelmed. In Jesus' name, amen.

SOMETHING TO TRY

Write the words "Be Still" somewhere you'll see them often. When life feels overwhelming, repeat those words to yourself and remember how those words calmed the storm in Mark 4:39.

THE TAKEAWAY

Jesus is our steady companion in an unsteady world. We can find peace in our storms because of the God who holds our faith.

POST 50

On Purpose and for a Purpose

The world around us can be overwhelming.

The constant cycle of news and social media fills our minds with everything that's wrong. Environmental catastrophe, animal extinction, racial injustice, the oppression of women, child poverty . . . We hear about it all, and it feels like we can't do anything to help. We're not in charge, and our voices are too small.

You might wonder, *How can I be an effective activist when there are so many problems clamoring for my attention*?

I (Kristel) once struggled with this very question.

The Random Facts of Your Life Aren't So Random

Did you know God made us all unique? Have you ever considered that God did that on purpose?

When I looked at my own story, I realized there were some very specific things God was calling me to. You see, I come from an immigrant family. We came to the US from Latin America. I was raised in Miami, one of the most densely immigrant-populated cities in the country. I grew up bilingual, speaking English and Spanish. For a long time, these felt like random facts about my life—nothing of much importance. I couldn't see how my story had anything to do with God's story. Surely, God didn't care about all that. Didn't God see us all the same anyway?

But as I embraced my ethnicity, culture, and migration story, I began to see how I could speak into situations from a unique perspective. I had something to say about immigration. I had something to say about racial diversity. My life experiences and my faith taught me that immigrants matter to God because we are made in God's image. Immigrants bring value and wisdom. Immigrants experience God personally and profoundly and have unique insights about God to share with local believers.

My life experiences and faith taught me that God values diversity and that we should strive to celebrate the unique ways God made us, which include our skin color, hair texture, culture, and language. God sees everything that makes us who we are and loves every creative detail.

Yes, we are equal in the eyes of God, but we are not the same. Unity doesn't mean *uniformity*; instead, we can find unity within our *diversity*.

Every time I thought about immigration and racial justice, my heart beat faster. I was passionate and deeply invested in making a difference in these two areas. I knew I could have maximum impact if I focused most of my attention on speaking up and writing about these issues and partnering with organizations working toward improving the lives of immigrants and repairing relationships between people of different ethnicities. I pored over my Bible and read books. I wanted to know everything I could about immigration and racial reconciliation from God's perspective.

Now, this doesn't mean I don't care about all the other causes in our world.

There are other people to whom God has given unique stories and passions. God has placed desires in their hearts to fight for orphans or remind those in prison they're deeply loved or clean up our beaches and rain forests. I'm so grateful that I don't have to fight for every form of justice on my own. I don't have to take on all the problems of the world. I can focus on the area God gave me, and I can trust others to focus on the areas God has given them.

That's why you are so needed. Your story. Your perspective. Your passion. Your concerns. Your gifts. They all have a place in God's story. You can use these to meet a need, answer a prayer, and share God's love in a hurting world.

READING GOD'S WORD

> You are a chosen people, a royal priesthood, a holy nation, God's special possession, that you may declare the praises of him who called you out of darkness into his wonderful light. (1 Peter 2:9 NIV)

> Serve each other according to the gift each person has received, as good managers of God's diverse gifts. (1 Peter 4:10)

REFLECT AND RESPOND

Journaling Questions

> What's your story? What's unique about your culture, family, or upbringing?

> What are you passionate about, and how can you use those passions to make a difference in the world?

> Where do you see God lining up your story with your passions?

Pray This Prayer

God, I praise you for the unique way you created me. Every quirk, every passion, every gift, every talent—you gave them to me on purpose and for a purpose. Help me to seek your will when using my gifts. Help me to see how I can seek justice in our world and partner with you to bring heaven to earth. In Jesus' name, amen.

SOMETHING TO TRY

Who around you is working for a cause that you feel passionately about? Reach out to them and ask how they got started. Spend time praying and seeking God's wisdom for how you can join the cause as well.

THE TAKEAWAY

Your passions, ethnicity, culture, and gifts are not random or accidental. God has uniquely created you with intent and purpose for the good of the world.

POST 51

Our Stories—and Purposes—Are Interconnected

> We must understand that the highest form of freedom carries with it the greatest measure of discipline.
>
> César Chávez[1]

Freedom requires discipline.

You might be thinking, *Way to take freedom and strap expectations on it. I get enough of that already.*

But that's not where we're going with this! In our society, we're mostly taught to believe that our own freedom is what counts—and by *freedom*, we often mean a big bucketful of ideas about personal choices and rights, including the right to basically do "whatever I want because it's my life."

Your Life Matters More Than You Know

"It's my life" isn't untrue, but it's not the whole story. Your life is so much more than just *yours*. And it matters much more than you know.

Here's an example. César Chávez became a leader of a huge farm-worker movement started by Filipino and Latino immigrants in the mid-1900s, organizing field laborers to advocate for rights to basic dignity and decent pay. These things might seem like no-brainers to us today, but at the time, there were few laws protecting workers' rights. This meant exploitation and overwork were commonplace. Chávez and other activists like Dolores Huerta were driven to fight for more freedoms because of the injustices they experienced and also by their faith in God. Prayer and worship were central to their activism.

But why would Chávez say, "The highest form of freedom carries with it the greatest measure of discipline"?

Discipline reminds us that we're never acting all on our own. What we do, watch, eat, buy, wear, share, throw away—it all matters. Our faith helps us see both freedom and discipline as part of a bigger story that realizes what we do with our lives impacts all the people around us. Our families and friends for sure, but even the people we don't think about very often—like maybe the ones who pick our strawberries in the springtime or clean our schools every evening.

When you put your life into the pages of a bigger story, you become mindful of how your individual story keeps crisscrossing others' stories. And that might mean:

You stop doing something because it hurts someone else.
You start doing something because it helps someone else.
You think twice about how you spend your money.
You pay attention to what you're throwing away.
You look another human in the eyes because they deserve to be seen.

All those actions take discipline—the discipline to see that we are responsible for one another's well-being.

Your life matters so much more than you realize—because your life is interconnected with so many other lives. We belong to one another.

READING GOD'S WORD

Christ is just like the human body—a body is a unit and has many parts; and all the parts of the body are one body, even though there are many. . . .

So the eye can't say to the hand, "I don't need you," or in turn, the head can't say to the feet, "I don't need you." Instead, the parts of the body that people think are the weakest are the most necessary. The parts of the body that we think are less honorable are the ones we honor the most. The private parts of our body that aren't presentable are the ones that are given the most dignity. The parts of our body that are presentable don't need this. But God has put the body together, giving greater honor to the part with less honor so that there won't be division in the body and so the parts might have mutual concern for each other. If one part suffers, all the parts suffer with it; if one part gets the glory, all the parts celebrate with it. You are the body of Christ and parts of each other. (1 Corinthians 12:12, 21–27)

REFLECT AND RESPOND

Journaling Questions

What do you think of the idea that freedom and discipline are bound together? Can you think of examples in history or in your own life where this is true?

How have you experienced the connectedness of "the body of Christ" through the actions of other believers?

How can you use your freedom for the sake of others?

Pray This Prayer

God, thank you for all the freedoms I enjoy in my life and for everything that makes those freedoms possible. Help me to see that my freedom is connected with others' and to live with the kind of discipline that helps set others free. In Jesus' name, amen.

SOMETHING TO TRY

Think through your past day or so. Try to imagine the people you came into contact with—maybe even make a list. Now imagine the people you didn't notice, or didn't directly see, who were also part of your day. The person who delivered packages to your door. The person who made your fast-food order. You get the idea.

Pick a few people in your orbit—whether you know their names or not—and pray for them for the next week. Ask God to open your eyes to see how your lives are connected.

THE TAKEAWAY

Your story matters not only for you but also for others.

POST 52

We're Better Together

Group projects. You love 'em or you hate 'em. I (Kristel) was never a fan.

Oh sure, it started out exciting enough, especially if I was grouped with friends, but inevitably people would slack from their responsibilities. Or they wouldn't complete their part of the project to my liking. Or they wouldn't complete it at all. Depending on someone else for my grade didn't sound like a good time to me.

Maybe that's one of the reasons I loved writing so much. It was mostly a solitary activity. I could sit in my room with my journal and a pen and create stories without input from anyone else. I was free to let my imagination run wild without imposition. I loved it so much that when I got older, I became a freelance writer.

My introverted self loved being alone with my computer, typing away. I didn't have to rely on anyone to complete my writing assignments. I could choose the work I wanted to take on and work at my own pace. It was great!

Not Meant to Go It Alone

Well, it was great until it wasn't. It didn't take long for me to start craving a writing community. I felt so alone and wanted to check in with other people who shared my love for writing and understood the ebb and flow of the work. I needed others to commiserate with me. I needed a group where we could cheer one another on and provide tips. I needed kindred spirits.

Thankfully, in the age of the internet, I soon found the group I was looking for. While we lived all across the continent and had various backgrounds and areas of interest with writing, we shared two things: we were all young moms and we were all writers.

Through this group, I found the community I was looking for. We checked in with one another throughout the day, shared when writing jobs became available, recommended each other to editors, and critiqued one another's work so we could perfect our craft. I realized then that writing didn't have to be a solitary activity—in fact, it was way more fun and fruitful with others along for the ride.

I've held on to this notion as I've gotten older. My goal is always to be on the lookout for people who share my passion and purpose so that I can invite them to work together in some way. When I see a young writer who is just starting out, I invite them to have coffee and talk about writing. I share opportunities with them to be mentored and develop their skills.

I also take this approach in my ministry work. On our team we have people with various strengths, and I'm glad about that! Some are visionaries, some like to organize tasks, some like to work directly with people, and some get excited about data and spreadsheets. I love giving people the freedom to be who they are and work in their strengths. When we all come together, we make a pretty great team.

I didn't always see the value in being part of a team, but now that I've experienced it, I can't deny that it's worth it. Yes, it takes time, intentionality, and hard work, but if everyone is "all in" and brings their unique gifts to the table, we can be better together.

READING GOD'S WORD

Certainly the body isn't one part but many. If the foot says, "I'm not part of the body because I'm not a hand," does that mean it's not part of the body? If the ear says, "I'm not part of the body because I'm not an eye," does that mean it's not part of the body? If the whole body were an eye, what would happen to the hearing? And if the whole body were an ear, what would happen to the sense of smell? But as it is, God has placed each one of the parts in the body just like he wanted. If all were one and the same body part, what would happen to the body? But as it is, there are many parts but one body. (1 Corinthians 12:14–20)

Two are better than one because they have a good return for their hard work. (Ecclesiastes 4:9)

REFLECT AND RESPOND

Journaling Questions

> What's your experience with group work or being part of a team? What's good about it, and what's challenging about it?

> When you read 1 Corinthians 12:14–20, what stands out to you? Why is every part important?

Pray This Prayer

God, thank you for the gift of community. Thank you for the gift of people who share my passions. Help me to connect with others in my purpose. In Jesus' name, amen.

SOMETHING TO TRY

What are you passionate about? What's something you want to try? How do you want to explore your purpose? Research a group that does something you're interested in or passionate about and join! It could be an after-school club, a nonprofit organization, or a local church group.

THE TAKEAWAY

Your purpose can get stronger when you practice it with others.

POST 53

Making a Difference by Helping Others

> I want to make a difference in people's lives, not necessarily like a big world-changing type of thing, but so that people will think, "Oh, wow, that was kind," or "that was cool for her to do."
>
> Sue

Making a difference in the world is a high priority for teenagers. Most teens want to leave a positive mark in some way. Maybe you've felt like this too.

One way that many teens are doing this is by helping others.

In his Boy Scout troop, church, and family, Steve's desire is to "help as many people in as many ways as I can. . . . Whether it is talking to someone who needs to get something off their chest or helping someone move stuff out of their house, I find purpose any time and any place I can help someone else."

Arthur describes those moments when he feels he's doing what he is meant to do: "It's when I'm teaching people. I never feel stressed when somebody at school comes to me for help learning music or math they can't grasp on their own."

Janelle serves as a leader in her school's Black Student Union. In that role, she spearheaded a campaign on African American mental health struggles.

Daniel is a junior who experienced homelessness for a year when his dad was ill and unable to work. Daniel is mindful of the kids who are homeless in his neighborhood. He rattled off the effects of homelessness—ranging from pollution to crime—that he had seen and encountered himself. Now that Daniel's family can afford an apartment, he's raising money to help those who are homeless, picking up trash to keep the streets cleaner, and advocating with city officials for more homeless shelters.

How Can You Help Others?

What sticks out in these various stories is that teens are tapping into their passions when helping others. Whether it's homelessness, mental health, or tutoring—teens aren't trying to do everything for everyone. They are focusing on what they love.

Making a difference doesn't have to be "a big world-changing type of thing," as Sue pointed out. You can make a difference in *your* circle of influence.

So when you think about how you want to make a difference in the world, instead of getting overwhelmed with the prospects, think of how you already enjoy helping people. It could be as simple as assisting with chores or letting someone borrow your pen. When we help people, their burdens are lifted and they feel seen and loved.

READING GOD'S WORD

Carry each other's burdens and so you will fulfill the law of Christ. (Galatians 6:2)

REFLECT AND RESPOND

Journaling Questions

> How do you like to help others?

> What do you like about helping others?

> What's one way you can use your story, life experience, or passions to help others?

Pray This Prayer

God, thank you for the opportunity to help others in big and small ways. It all matters. Help me to discover my passions so I can make a difference in this world by helping others. In Jesus' name, amen.

SOMETHING TO TRY

This week, offer to help someone in a small and simple way. Ideas include:

- Take your neighbor's dog for a walk.
- Wash laundry for a family member.

- Help a friend study for a test.
- Buy a coffee for a tired family member.

THE TAKEAWAY

You can make a difference by helping in ways you're already wired to help.

POST 54

Navigating America's Complicated Racial Past and Present

Race in America has a complicated history.

It's a history fraught with hatred, cruelty, and prejudice.

Depending on your own racial background, it may be all too easy to think these complications are a thing of the past—the days of antebellum slavery or the civil rights movement of the 1960s. Or you may be well-aware these conflicts are just as active today as ever, in your life and the lives of others. There is still so much work to be done.

This became evident in an explosive way in May 2020 with the murder of George Floyd. The US, with the entire world, was already reeling from a pandemic when a cell phone video posted by seventeen-year-old Darnella Frazier went viral. The world watched as a Black man pleaded for his life for over nine minutes while a white police officer kneeled on his neck. Though several bystanders shouted concerns and Floyd himself pleaded for breath, the officer refused to move. Eventually, George Floyd's body went limp.

What Does This Mean for Christ Followers?

The Bible is filled with stories of conflict and war between people from different nations, ethnic groups, and tribes. But God's desire has always been to create *one* family made up of *every* nation, tribe, and language (Revelation 7:9). A beautifully diverse family that is united even in their differences.

In Genesis, God promised to make Abraham the father of many nations (17:5). Thanks to complicated family dynamics, this became true through both Ishmael and Isaac.

Throughout the Old Testament, there are stories of God calling on Israel to be a light to the nations so that God could redeem them.

The prophet Jonah was specifically sent out to preach to the Ninevites and call them to repentance. He had a detour in the belly of a fish, but he made it eventually.

In the New Testament, Jesus fulfills God's desire. He breaks down the wall of hostility, bringing Jews and Gentiles together (Ephesians 2:14).

Now God's intent for a multiethnic family is fulfilled. It's a family that displays unity without uniformity—unity within its diversity.

But humans are still flawed. We hold on to our fears and prejudices. We forget to walk in the freedom that has been given to us. We try to rebuild the wall that has been destroyed.

As Christ followers, we must follow the way of Jesus. We can be honest about the racial history in our country and world. We can lament over the mistreatment of people of color in the US. We can repent for any way we may have participated in this pattern in our culture, knowingly or unknowingly.

In the face of racism and prejudice, we must choose to put on compassion, humility, gentleness, patience, and love. We must ask God to bond us together in unity—unity that does not erase our differences but embraces them.

It's not an easy task.

There is an enemy who would love for us to stay separated. The sin of racism tries to work its way in to cause division. It's necessary that we stay alert, pray, and actively push back against racism. We do this by living with humility, forgiveness, and gratitude for the uniqueness of each person. We do this by speaking up and banding together against all forms of racism.

Diversity is beautiful in God's sight. May we have eyes to see people the way God sees them: with profound love and respect. Part of the family.

READING GOD'S WORD

> Therefore, as God's choice, holy and loved, put on compassion, kindness, humility, gentleness, and patience. Be tolerant with each other and, if someone has a complaint against anyone, forgive each other. As the Lord forgave you, so also forgive each other. And over all these things put on love, which is the perfect bond of unity. The peace of Christ must control your hearts—a peace into which you were called in one body. And be thankful people. The word of Christ must live in you richly. Teach and warn each other with all wisdom by singing psalms, hymns, and spiritual songs. Sing to God with gratitude in your hearts. Whatever you do, whether in speech or action, do it all in the name of the Lord Jesus and give thanks to God the Father through him. (Colossians 3:12–17)

> For he himself is our peace, who has made the two groups one and has destroyed the barrier, the dividing wall of hostility. (Ephesians 2:14 NIV)

REFLECT AND RESPOND

Journaling Questions

> Name some of your own experiences with racism in your life so far.

How can you actively push back against racism in your community?

What does unity look like to you?

Pray This Prayer

God, racism is a grave evil. It can be difficult to navigate the racial reality of our world, but help me to be a light in the darkness. Help me to stand up for love, unity, inclusivity, and diversity. In Jesus' name, amen.

SOMETHING TO TRY

Is there an ethnic group you don't know much about? In the face of what's unknown, we can make up stories or believe stereotypes. We might even develop unhealthy fears against certain groups.

Take some time to research an ethnic group you're unfamiliar with. Learn about their culture, customs, and traditions. This could be your first step in restoration across races.

THE TAKEAWAY

Navigating the racial reality of our world can be messy and difficult, but we are empowered by God to show love and stand against racism.

POST 55

Building Cultural Bridges

In part 1 of this book, we talked about Claudia and her attempt to build cultural bridges between her friends of different ethnic groups. In today's world, we have so many opportunities to build cultural bridges.

But why? What's the purpose of building these bridges? And what makes these bridges last long-term?

Learning about other cultures is fun. Creating harmony between different types of people seems like a worthy cause. Ultimately, however, we build cultural bridges not just for fun or sociological reasons but for biblical reasons.

Jesus, the Ultimate Bridge

God always intended a multiethnic global family. God loves all of creation and calls it good. God desires for us to live in unity bonded by love.

Jesus came to fulfill that desire for one multiethnic family. The early church, for the most part, understood that. The gospel was being preached in Jerusalem and Judea and Samaria and beyond (Acts 1:8).

British theologian N. T. Wright said in a recent interview:

> The church from the beginning . . . always was a multicultural, multiethnic, multipolychrome, multilingual organization. Like in Revelation,

> a great company of many nations and kindreds and tribes and tongues, all together praising God and the Lamb. That's the vision of the church in the New Testament. We, in the last four or five hundred years, have colluded with division down ethnic lines without even realizing just how unbiblical we were being. We'd taken our eye off that ball and were looking instead at theories of salvation, about going to heaven.[1]

Jesus bridged humanity to God and humanity to one another—across ethnicities, cultures, and languages. The early church had a picture of Revelation 7:9 in mind—people from every nation worshiping God together.

As Wright says, we took our eye off the ball. All of a sudden, other aspects of the faith became more important than ethnic unity. We created lines and divisions where none should have existed.

But God is still at work through his people here on earth. Through the Spirit's enabling power, we can return to God's vision for a united multiethnic family. We can be God's witnesses on this earth and build bridges so people across cultures can come together.

This is the restoration of God's original design and the fulfilling of Jesus' purpose into which we are invited.

Bringing people together is part of your purpose. How you live it out specifically in your daily life will be unique—but we are all working toward the same goal.

READING GOD'S WORD

> You will receive power when the Holy Spirit has come upon you, and you will be my witnesses in Jerusalem, in all Judea and Samaria, and to the end of the earth. (Acts 1:8)

> The Lord isn't slow to keep his promise, as some think of slowness, but he is patient toward you, not wanting anyone to perish but all to change their hearts and lives. (2 Peter 3:9)

> Therefore, go and make disciples of all nations. (Matthew 28:19)

REFLECT AND RESPOND

Journaling Questions

> Who is someone in your life or in history who has built cultural bridges? How did they do it?

> What's the value in building these kinds of bridges?

> Who is one person from a different culture or ethnicity than yours whom you can build a bridge to?

Pray This Prayer

God, you call us to build cultural bridges because you desire for all people to be included in your multiethnic family. Thank you for giving us your Spirit to empower us in our purpose to build bridges. It's an honor and privilege to join you on your mission. In Jesus' name, amen.

SOMETHING TO TRY

Would you say that all potatoes are the same? Maybe!

Grab a bag of potatoes and take out four. Examine each one—note the varying color tones, bumps, and spores. You will probably find that each potato is actually quite unique.

Remember this the next time you try to lump an entire cultural group together.

THE TAKEAWAY

We all share a role in the same purpose that Jesus fulfilled—to build cultural bridges. How we each live out this purpose will be unique, but it's all through the Spirit's power.

POST 56

How What's Tough Can Transform You

How can I be a leader on campus without risking an election loss?

That was a driving question for me (Kara) in tenth grade. I hated failure in general. Public failure—through an event like an election—was the worst.

As a sophomore, I applied for and was selected by teachers to serve as class secretary.

In eleventh grade, I interviewed and was chosen by the student senate to be secretary of our school's student body.

But in twelfth grade, I wanted to be student body president. That meant I had no choice but to run in an election.

My friends and I gave away handfuls of candy, all plastered with creative campaign slogans. While I still feared the humiliation of an election loss, so many underclassmen promised to vote for me that I thought I had a good chance of winning.

That hope disintegrated as soon as the results were posted. Not only did I not win but I came in third—out of three candidates.

This was no flubbed interview behind closed doors. This felt like public shaming. I needed someplace to hide.

So I drove home, ran upstairs to my bedroom, slammed the door, and curled under the covers. I had never tried this hard and failed this big.

How could I ever face my friends, let alone the entire school?

A few hours later, I left the safety of my bed and went downstairs to hugs from my mom, stepdad, and younger brother. That helped. But I still felt discontented and disoriented.

Until Mike and Kristi, my youth pastor and small group leader, came by to talk.

They spent time listening to how I felt and prayed with me. I was especially surprised when Mike predicted, "Someday you're going to catch a vision for youth ministry. And then watch out."

A few months later, I started hanging around our church more and even joined the student leadership team. (To my relief, no election was required.)

By the end of my senior year, I was pretty much running that team.

During my college summers, I served in the youth ministry as a volunteer and then as a paid intern.

Mike was right. During college and seminary, God gave me a vision for young people. And thirty years later, I'm still in youth ministry. If I had won that election, I'm not sure I would be serving with teenagers and getting to know you through this devotional. God's plans were different than I expected but so much better.

The Best Plans

During the era when the Jews were living in captivity first under the Egyptians, then the Babylonians, and finally the Persians, they understandably wondered where God was and if God was listening. To encourage the Israelites with God's ability to transform what is tough, the prophet Jeremiah said to them: "'For I know the plans I have for you,' declares the Lord, 'plans to prosper you and not to harm you, plans to give you hope and a future'" (Jeremiah 29:11 NIV).

There's a lot of good news in verses 11–13!

God has plans for us.

Those plans are the best.

When we call on God, God listens to us.

When we look for God, we can find God. God isn't playing hide-and-seek with us.

READING GOD'S WORD

> "For I know the plans I have for you," declares the LORD, "plans to prosper you and not to harm you, plans to give you hope and a future. Then you will call on me and come and pray to me, and I will listen to you. You will seek me and find me when you seek me with all your heart." (Jeremiah 29:11–13 NIV)

REFLECT AND RESPOND

Journaling Questions

> What's your current top struggle or loss?

> How might God be using that struggle to prepare you for the next step on God's path? How might what is tough be used to transform you?

> What would it look like for you to trust in God's plan for your life right now?

Pray This Prayer

God, while a big part of me wishes that life was easy all the time, I'm grateful for how you use challenges to change us. Please use the tough times I face to grow my trust in you. May I learn all that you want me to learn, and become all that you want me to become, through the difficulties I face. Thank you that you are with me in all times—both good and bad. In Jesus' name, amen.

SOMETHING TO TRY

Whatever you're facing, is there a wise friend or caring adult with whom you could discuss it? Just as I felt a whole lot better when I talked over my election loss with Mike and Kristi, you likely will too.

THE TAKEAWAY

Loss can feel like the end sometimes, but God can turn loss around for our ultimate good.

POST 57

Knowing When to Say Yes and When to Say No

Part of discovering your purpose is knowing when to say yes and when to say no. If you want to find your purpose and develop the skills needed to work toward your purpose, you will have to learn how to focus your time and attention.

If that sounds hard, we're with you! But hear us out.

Sometimes you think saying yes to every opportunity is what you need to do in order to lean into your purpose—but if you say yes to everything, sooner or later you will burn out.

This is something that Jesus knew well. During his earthly ministry, Jesus was often followed by large crowds. They all wanted to hear him teach, and they clamored for his attention. Meeting those kinds of demands is exhausting. This is why Jesus instituted boundaries. While he said yes to many ministry opportunities—from healing the sick to meeting with people—he also knew when to say no.

Jesus knew that it was important to take time away from the crowds. He accepted his personal limits and took care of his personal needs. When he was hungry, he ate. When he was tired, he slept. He would often retreat to be alone with God the Father. Saying no allowed him to focus his time and guarded him from fatigue.

What about When Jesus Said Yes?

There were many times when Jesus said yes, but let's focus on one in particular. When Jesus was praying in the garden of Gethsemane before going to the cross, he said, "Father, if it's your will, take this cup of suffering away from me. However, not my will but your will must be done" (Luke 22:42).

Jesus understood that obedience means saying yes to God's will for our lives. In order to fulfill his ultimate purpose, Jesus had to say yes to what God had called him to do. It may not have been what others were expecting, but it was God's call. So he said yes.

The bottom line? Say a joyful and willing *yes* when the request seems to line up with God's will for your life and you have the capacity to do so. Say *no* to anything that will distract you from God's will for your life (you probably don't have the capacity anyway).

You may not think you know God's will all the time, and that's fine. Don't stress it. Go with what you know so far. As you figure out when to say yes and when to say no, and mean it, God's purpose for you will unfold.

READING GOD'S WORD

> Let your *yes* mean yes, and your *no* mean no. Anything more than this comes from the evil one. (Matthew 5:37)

> Your speech should always be gracious and sprinkled with insight so that you may know how to respond to every person. (Colossians 4:6)

REFLECT AND RESPOND

Journaling Questions

> What's hard about saying yes? What's easy about saying yes?

What's hard about saying no? What's easy about saying no?

What's one way you can align your yes or no with God's purpose for your life?

Pray This Prayer

God, as I discover your purpose for my life, help me to be wise with my time and attention. Guide me in when to say yes and when to say no. Help me to stand firm in the boundaries that will best serve in helping me stick to my purpose. In Jesus' name, amen.

SOMETHING TO TRY

Take a look at all your commitments—the things you've said yes to. Is there anything on that list that needs to be a no? Take some time to think and pray about what needs to be a yes and what needs to be a no.

THE TAKEAWAY

Knowing when to say yes and when to say no helps you set boundaries and concentrate on what leads you toward God's purpose for you.

POST 58

How to Bring Good News with Our Feet

Are you wearing shoes? Take them off.

Really. In fact, take off your socks too. This is a barefoot-required post.

Take a few moments to look at your feet. What are they like? Where have they been? What story do they tell?

When I (Brad) think about my feet, I think about my dad. For the last twenty years of his life, he was a paraplegic—he couldn't feel or move his legs or feet, so he used a wheelchair. In contrast, mine have run a marathon.

I also think about my grandma. Her feet spent most all of her ninety-seven years of life grounded on a farm in central Kentucky—the same farm where my mom grew up and where I grew up—walking cow paths and wading creeks. But my feet have also tramped across the country and the world, now rambling where I live in Southern California.

The condition of our feet makes a difference in the way our story unfolds.

The choices available to us shape the literal paths our feet walk.

Up to now, life has mostly made those choices for you. Your body and its abilities, strengths, and struggles. Your ancestors, your parents, your teachers, your community. There are also the big forces that expand or limit our choices such as family finances, race, class, and immigration status—not to mention local geography, ideals, and politics. So many factors!

Going Somewhere

So what happens when more choices are up to you?

That might sound stressful.

Let me lower the pressure here: today we're going to think less about *where* you're going to go and more about *how*.

Look at your feet again. What makes your feet look either good or not so good? It depends on who is setting the standard, right? The prophet Isaiah had something to say about that. In one of his writings, Isaiah said our feet look good—even beautiful—*when they bring good news*: "How beautiful upon the mountains are the feet of a messenger who proclaims peace, who brings good news, who proclaims salvation" (Isaiah 52:7).

Isaiah is using the image of a message bearer on foot, coming over mountains across the borders from another land. The messenger might actually be yelling "GOOD NEWS! GOOD NEWS!" to anyone who can hear. For the people in Jerusalem at that time, it meant the return of their relatives from exile. It signaled a new era, and even the sense that God's presence was returning to the land.

That all sounds long ago and far away. What could it mean for us now?

Feet still bring good news. And people still need good news in their lives—in a big way. You may feel a little awkward running down the street yelling "GOOD NEWS!" to strangers. That's okay. The "news behind the news" to Isaiah's listeners was that God is bringing his reign—God's kingdom—into our midst. That's what God was up to then—and still what God is up to now.

My story could be a beautiful story whether my feet had mostly stayed in the same community my entire life like my grandmother or my feet had stopped working altogether like my dad's. Our feet are beautiful because of the good news—the way we live out God's message in our big decisions and everyday choices.

In other words, it's not so much *where* your feet are going but *how*. When you walk with good-looking feet, you're living out God's purpose for you.

READING GOD'S WORD

> How beautiful upon the mountains
> are the feet of a messenger
> who proclaims peace,
> who brings good news,
> who proclaims salvation,
> who says to Zion, "Your God rules!" (Isaiah 52:7)

> As shoes for your feet put on whatever will make you ready to proclaim the gospel of peace. (Ephesians 6:15 NRSV)

REFLECT AND RESPOND

Journaling Questions

When have you experienced someone who had beautiful feet—who brought good news into your life?

Look at your feet again. Where have they been? Where are they going? What stories do they tell?

> Where might God want to take your feet? How can you go in a way that truly carries good news to others?

Pray This Prayer

> *Lord, you made my feet. You know where they've been and where they will go. This is all too big for me to imagine or control. Help me today to be someone who brings good news through the way I live—in my words, actions, and decisions—right now. And help me to imagine a future in which my feet carry hope wherever they tread. In Jesus' name, amen.*

SOMETHING TO TRY

Write "GOOD NEWS" on your foot—you can decide which foot, where, how big, and if you want to decorate it. If you're a minimalist, just use the initials "GN." Up to you. Here's the point: whenever you see your mark this week, let it be a reminder that wherever your feet go, you can bring good news to the world around you.

THE TAKEAWAY

Your feet are beautiful because of the good news—the way you live out God's message in your big decisions and everyday choices.

POST 59

Finding Contentment

> You cannot have everything. I want to be satisfied with what I have and able to appreciate those who love and surround me. Most people define happiness as having everything you want, but sometimes that still feels empty. For me, being able to love everybody in my life is the best happiness.
>
> Arthur

"I can do all things through Christ who gives me strength."

Have you heard that saying before? It's based on a popular Bible verse, Philippians 4:13, and used freely in Christian circles.

I (Kristel) remember hearing that phrase when I was younger and picturing a battle scene in my mind. I had armor and a huge sword, and I was running into a fight—a fight I was going to win because God had given me strength.

But actually, that's not what that verse is about at all. When you zoom out and read the verse in the context of the verses before and after it in Scripture, you find that it's about *contentment*. About being okay with what you have and what you don't—or with who you are and who you're not.

Paul, the writer of this letter to his friends in Philippi, is thanking the Philippian church for taking care of him. He expresses his belief that he can be content no matter the circumstance because he is getting to fulfill God's purpose for his life of building up the church.

I know a thing or two about contentment . . . and discontentment.

For many years, I felt frustrated with my life. It didn't seem like anything was going my way. I couldn't find contentment, and it made me feel guilty. Was I not living out Philippians 4:13? Paul said he could find contentment no matter what. Why couldn't I?

One night, as I sat around a fire with my small group from church, my friend told me, "Maybe you're feeling a holy discontent."

I had to think about that. I didn't want to mistakenly claim that I was righteous in my feelings if I wasn't. I had to spend intentional time in prayer asking God to show me why I was unhappy and how I could find the happiness I was searching for.

Becoming Content in Your Purpose

After a lot of prayer and conversations with people I trusted, I concluded that I wasn't living in God's purpose for my life—this was the source of my discontentment. And when you're not living out God's purpose for your life, you won't find happiness either.

God had created me in a specific way, and I knew how I wanted to live out God's purpose for me. There were circumstances, however, that were preventing me from doing that.

Little by little, I began to make changes and seek opportunities that would align with my passions and skills and what I thought was God's purpose for me. Those changes weren't big or flashy. And they didn't make me famous or rich. But they were fulfilling. And eventually, I became content.

READING GOD'S WORD

I rejoiced greatly in the Lord that at last you renewed your concern for me. Indeed, you were concerned, but you had no opportunity to show it. I am not saying this because I am in need, for I have learned to be content whatever the circumstances. I know what it is to be in need, and I know what it is to have plenty. I have learned the secret of being content in any and every situation, whether well fed or hungry, whether living in plenty or in want. I can do all this through him who gives me strength. (Philippians 4:10–13 NIV)

REFLECT AND RESPOND

Journaling Questions

What do you think your purpose is?

What opportunities can you seek that will lead you to your purpose?

Why is purpose an important part of contentment?

Pray This Prayer

God, help me to be content in any circumstance. I know that as long as I am walking in your purpose, I don't have to worry about fame, money, or recognition. I can be content knowing that I am fulfilling what you want for my life. I'm grateful for your faithfulness. In Jesus' name, amen.

SOMETHING TO TRY

Gratitude plays a big role in contentment. Paul demonstrated this in his letter to the Philippians when he thanked them for the gifts they sent.

What are you thankful for?

Make a gratitude list of your own. If you love to draw, it could be fun to draw the different things you're thankful for. Give it a try!

THE TAKEAWAY

When you live into God's purpose, you can find contentment, no matter the circumstances.

POST 60

The World Needs You to Come Alive

> I feel like I belong now—how do I say this—in this world. I feel like now I have a purpose.
>
> Armando

Are you really *alive*?

Twentieth-century writer and theologian Howard Thurman once told a young person, "Don't ask yourself what the world needs. Ask yourself what makes you come alive and then go do that. Because what the world needs is people who have come alive."[1]

What does it mean to come alive? Is that a trick question?

Of course, if you're reading this right now, you're alive. That's good news! You're not a zombie.

Actually, you are a small miracle—the fact that your heart is beating, your lungs are expanding and contracting, your brain is running a massive network of neurological wonder so complex that the world's best scientists still don't fully understand it. When you stop to think about it, being alive is kind of mind-blowing.

But there's more.

Thurman was speaking to the dilemma of purpose: *What should I do? How can I make a difference? How will my life matter in the world?* This kind of wondering can turn into worrying. It can make your brain hurt.

Being Fully You

Instead of agonizing over figuring out the "one thing" that you were meant to do or that the world most needs you to do, Thurman offers a freeing alternative: be fully alive.

Thurman loved praying, reflecting on Scripture, pastoring people, teaching and writing about God, and acting out God's heart for justice in the world. He didn't see these as separate pursuits but all part of one consistent stream—following Jesus. And it all made him feel fully alive because he was being himself while he followed Jesus.

What makes you feel fully alive? Maybe the following are clues to what it means for you to come alive:

When do you feel most truly yourself?
What brings you joy?
When do you have the most energy?
When do you sense God's presence the most?

Jesus said that he came into the world so we may "have life, and have it abundantly" (John 10:10 NRSV). Life to the full. Life not just later in heaven but here and now on earth. Flourishing. Being whole.

Coming alive is always what God has wanted for you. And when you feel fully alive, you are being who the world needs you to be.

READING GOD'S WORD

Jesus spoke again, "I assure you that I am the gate of the sheep. All who came before me were thieves and outlaws, but the sheep didn't listen to them. I am the gate. Whoever enters through me will be saved. They will come in and go out and find pasture. The thief enters only to steal, kill, and destroy. I came so that they could have life—indeed, so that they could live life to the fullest." (John 10:7–10)

But because of his great love for us, God, who is rich in mercy, made us alive with Christ even when we were dead in transgressions—it is by grace you have been saved. And God raised us up with Christ and seated us with him in the heavenly realms in Christ Jesus, in order that in the coming ages he might show the incomparable riches of his grace, expressed in his kindness to us in Christ Jesus. For it is by grace you have been saved, through faith—and this is not from yourselves, it is the gift of God—not by works, so that no one can boast. For we are God's handiwork, created in Christ Jesus to do good works, which God prepared in advance for us to do. (Ephesians 2:4–10 NIV)

REFLECT AND RESPOND

Journaling Questions

> Think about your own life for a moment—your physical, breathing, beating-heart, emotion-filled life. What are you grateful for? What is amazing to you about being alive?

> Consider what makes you feel like you're really alive—physically, emotionally, spiritually, mentally. Is it listening to your favorite music? Going for a run? Dreaming up a new graphic novel? Coding? Serving in an after-school tutoring center? Write some of your own ideas, and if you're not sure, list some things you think you'd like to try.

> How does the idea of "coming alive" help—or not help—when it comes to pressure about your future?

Pray This Prayer

Lord of life, thank you for making me and giving me life. Thank you for making me uniquely me—even for the things I don't like about myself sometimes. Give me discernment to see how you have made me and what it means for me to truly come alive. Help me to offer the gift of my full self to the world. In Jesus' name, amen.

Something to Try

Take time this week to do something that makes you feel truly alive. Pay attention to yourself: How do you feel before, during, and after? What do you enjoy most about the experience?

If you're not really sure when you feel most alive, that's okay. Keep your antenna up to catch signals when they come through.

THE TAKEAWAY

You don't have to have it all figured out. Start by coming alive.

Your Next Faithful Step

> A lot of people have their goals set, especially about their occupation. "I want to be this when I grow up" or "I want to be that . . ." Instead, I try to go with the flow, trusting God. I will be what God wants me to be—in ten years, in twenty years. I don't want to have a set path for my life, because I know that God may have something different for me. So what do I want to be when I grow up? I just want to be someone who has a relationship with God where I can trust God with anything and everything.
>
> Samuel

Wow, friend, you've made it to the close of this guide!

Now the rest of your story begins.

We are so grateful to have been your companions on this part of the journey. And we hope this book can be a resource you circle back through again whenever you need it.

To wrap up, we offer three reminders and a blessing.

First, the reminders. If we had to summarize all that we've said about identity, belonging, and purpose, we'd say this:

1. Jesus makes you ENOUGH.
2. You belong WITH God and God's people.
3. You can make a difference when you see your purpose as part of God's greater STORY.

With all that in mind, figuring out who you are, where you fit, and what to do with your life doesn't have to be so stressful. Using the tools you've picked up along the way in this book, your guiding question can be: *What's my next faithful step?*

Yes, we're ending where we began: with another question.

Your next faithful step might look as simple as calling a friend or as complicated as deciding what to do after high school. Whether you're wrestling with questions of identity, belonging, or purpose, you can approach your future with confidence, knowing that God's Spirit goes with you each step of the way.

A Final Blessing

We are leaving you with one final blessing, adapted from Ephesians 3:16–21. (This is definitely a passage we encourage you to find in your own Bible, mark up, screenshot, write out and stick to your wall—whatever helps you see it again and again.) We've added language of identity, belonging, and purpose to this blessing.

We can't think of a more appropriate prayer for you, so imagine us praying it out loud together over you right now.

> *May God strengthen you in your identity from the riches of God's glory through the Holy Spirit.*
>
> *May Christ live in your heart through faith.*
>
> *As a result of having strong roots in love, may you have the power to grasp love's width and length, height and depth, together with all believers—to know that you truly belong.*
>
> *May you know the love of Christ that is beyond knowledge so that you will be filled entirely with the fullness of God.*
>
> *Glory to God, who gives us purpose and who is able to do far beyond all that we could ask or imagine by the Spirit's power at work within us. Glory to God in the church and in Christ Jesus for all generations, forever and always!*
>
> *Amen.*

Acknowledgments

This book is the fruit of God's Spirit prompting us, bringing us together, and using a village of people around us to make it a reality! Our first and deepest gratitude goes to God, giver of all good gifts.

Special thanks to our editor, Stephanie Duncan Smith at Baker Books, and our agent, Greg Johnson at WordServe Literary, for urging us to move forward on this important project and for helping Kara and Brad discover Kristel as a gifted writing partner. From start to finish, Stephanie asked all the right questions and relentlessly kept us focused on teen readers. Our entire publishing team at Baker Books is just plain amazing. We are especially grateful to Eileen Hanson, Brianna DeWitt, and the rest of the marketing crew for laboring so cheerfully to bring this book into the world.

The research grounding this devotional is detailed in *3 Big Questions That Change Every Teenager*, and while we won't rename here all the people who touched that project, it's important to call out that neither book would exist without the twenty-seven diverse teenagers who generously shared their stories of identity, belonging, and purpose. In order to protect their confidentiality, we've given them aliases, but they are very real people with very sacred stories. We were equally dependent on the other members of the interview team, who spent well over one hundred hours asking questions and listening deeply: Kat Armas, Macy Davis, Tyler Greenway, Jennifer Guerra Aldana,

Garrison Hayes, Jane Hong-Guzmán de León, Helen Jun, and Andy Jung. To everyone who participated in interview transcription, analysis, literature review, advising, and synthesis, a hearty THANK YOU again.

The entire Fuller Youth Institute team has endlessly supported this project, and Kara and Brad are especially thankful to Yulee Lee and Jake Mulder for their partnership in senior leadership as well as the team members whose day-to-day work made this book launch possible: Macy Davis, Rachel Dodd, Mai Anh Hall, Nica Halula, Jennifer Hananouchi, Roslyn Hernández, Andy Jung, Issac Kim, John Kwok, Will Lewis, and Giovanny Panginda. Special thanks to Tim Galleher for helping us gather student-reader feedback to improve our first draft, and to Ahren Martinez and Jennifer Guerra Aldana for offering additional cultural review. We are so very grateful for the generous funders who make our research and resources possible, in particular Lilly Endowment Inc.

Crystal Chiang and the wizarding curriculum team at Orange Students dared to collaborate with us to take the findings from *3 Big Questions That Change Every Teenager* and develop middle and high school youth ministry curriculum called *The Big Questions*. We're so glad they did, and we hope leaders and students will find these resources partner well for deeper kingdom impact!

Kristel would especially like to thank her parents, Kristabel and Danilo Lopez, for all the sacrifices they made by immigrating to another country and for laying foundations of both faith and writing in her life. She also thanks the leadership at Transformation Church for their support, prayers, and encouragement—not only in this project but in daily ministry life.

Finally, eternal gratitude goes to our spouses, Dave Powell, Alex Acevedo, and Missy Griffin, for making writing possible—especially midpandemic. And huge thanks to our kids, whose feedback made this a better book and whose lives make us better people: Nathan, Krista, and Jessica Powell; Liam and Isabel Acevedo; and Anna, Kara, and Joel Griffin. This book is dedicated to your own journeys toward identity, belonging, and purpose.

Notes

Introduction

1. Martin B. Copenhaver, *Jesus Is the Question: The 307 Questions Jesus Asked and the 3 He Answered* (Nashville: Abingdon, 2014), xviii.

2. A word about Bible translations. Since the Bible was originally written in Hebrew, Aramaic, and Greek, every passage you read in English or any other language comes from a translation. For this book, we've chosen mostly to use the Common English Bible. When we use another translation, we'll add initials after the passage. That way, if you want to look it up, you'll know which translation we're using (or if you want to compare the same passage in different translations). Those initials include: ASV for the American Standard Version, CEV for the Contemporary English Version, CSB for the Christian Standard Bible, NIV for the New International Version, NLT for the New Living Translation, and NRSV for the New Revised Standard Version. Also, while we don't include translations in Spanish, Korean, or other languages beyond English in this book, we encourage you to look up passages in your family's first language as well!

Post 5 God's Intentional Design for Your Ethnicity

1. *Selena*, directed by Gregory Nava (Burbank, CA: Warner Bros. Pictures, 1997).

Post 12 You Are More Than Your Success

1. Timothy Keller, Twitter, November 8, 2019, 10:14 a.m., https://twitter.com/timkellernyc/status/1192822599002312704.

Post 15 Unplugging to Notice God

1. Adapted with permission from Kara Powell and Brad Griffin, *Sticky Faith Every Day: 8 Weeks of Noticing God More* (Pasadena, CA: Fuller Youth Institute, 2013).

Post 17 Your Voice Matters

1. *The Hunger Games*, directed by Gary Ross (Santa Monica, CA: Lionsgate, 2012).

Part 2 Where Do I Fit?

1. Brené Brown, *Braving the Wilderness: The Quest for True Belonging and the Courage to Stand Alone* (New York: Penguin Random House, 2017), 158.

Post 22 What Do Real Friendships Look Like?

1. Bridget Quinn, *She Votes: How U.S. Women Won Suffrage, and What Happened Next* (San Francisco: Chronicle Books, 2020), 49.
2. Penny Colman, *Elizabeth Cady Stanton and Susan B. Anthony: A Friendship That Changed the World* (New York: Henry Holt and Company, 2013), 130.

Post 29 How to Be a Peacemaker

1. Desmond Tutu, *An African Prayer Book* (New York: Crown Publishing, 2009), 80.
2. Desmond Tutu Quotes, BrainyQuote.com, accessed January 31, 2022, https://www.brainyquote.com/quotes/desmond_tutu_454135.
3. Desmond Tutu, *No Future Without Forgiveness* (New York: Penguin Random House, 2000), 255.
4. Desmond Tutu, quoted in "Marching for Peace and Justice," World Council of Churches, February 2, 2006, http://wcc2006.info/en/news-media/news/english-news/browse/1/article/469/marching-for-peace-and-ju.html.

Post 31 How Can Empathy Fuel Belonging?

1. Adapted from former Fuller Seminary professor David W. Augsburger, *Caring Enough to Hear and Be Heard* (Ventura, CA: Regal Books, 1982), 12.

Post 35 Being a True Neighbor

1. Gregory Boyle, *Barking at the Choir: The Power of Radical Kinship* (New York: Simon & Schuster, 2017), 3.
2. Miles McPherson, sermon delivered at Mosaix Conference, 2019, https://multiethnic.church/.

Post 38 Lamenting Our Losses Together

1. Portions of this devotion adapted with permission from Kara Powell and Brad Griffin, *Sticky Faith Every Day: 8 Weeks of Noticing God More* (Pasadena, CA: Fuller Youth Institute, 2013).

Post 39 Celebrating with Others

1. *Encanto*, directed by Jared Bush, Byron Howard, and Charise Castro Smith (Burbank, CA: Walt Disney Animation Studios, 2021).

Post 40 Connecting with God's Presence Anytime

1. Portions of this devotion adapted with permission from Kara Powell and Brad Griffin, *Sticky Faith Every Day: 8 Weeks of Noticing God More* (Pasadena, CA: Fuller Youth Institute, 2013).

Part 3 What Difference Can I Make?

1. Alasdair MacIntyre, *After Virtue* (Notre Dame, IN: University of Notre Dame Press, 1981), 216.

Post 46 Putting Faith into Action

1. Georges Gorrée and Jean Barbier, eds., *The Love of Christ: Spiritual Counsels by Mother Teresa* (New York: Harper & Row, 1982).
2. Mother Teresa and Lucinda Vardey, *Mother Teresa: A Simple Path* (New York: Ballantine Books, 1995), xxxii.

Post 51 Our Stories—and Purposes—Are Interconnected

1. Kekla Magoon, *Cesar Chavez: Crusader for Labor Rights* (Edina, MN: ABDO Publishing, 2011), 33.

Post 55 Building Cultural Bridges

1. Jerry Bowyer, "An Interview with N.T. Wright on How Christ Bridges Ethnic, Gender, Class Divisions," *Christian Post*, October 22, 2021, https://www.christianpost.com/news/an-interview-with-nt-wright-on-how-christ-bridges-diviisions.html.

Post 60 The World Needs You to Come Alive

1. Gil Bailie, *Violence Unveiled: Humanity at the Crossroads* (New York: Crossroad Publishing, 1995), xv.

Kara Powell, PhD, is Chief of Leadership Formation and Executive Director of the Fuller Youth Institute at Fuller Theological Seminary. A Youth and Family Strategist for Orange and regular conference speaker, Kara has authored or coauthored many books, including *3 Big Questions That Change Every Teenager*. Kara and her husband, Dave, have three teenage and young adult children.

Kristel Acevedo is the Spiritual Formation Director at Transformation Church in Indian Land, South Carolina. Originally from Miami, Florida, she is a writer and speaker focused on discipleship, Bible study, and multiethnic ministry. Kristel and her husband, Alex, have two young children.

Brad M. Griffin is Senior Director of Content for the Fuller Youth Institute and a youth pastor at Mountainside Communion. He's a speaker and the coauthor of over a dozen books, including *3 Big Questions That Change Every Teenager*. Brad and his wife, Missy, live in Southern California and have three teenage and young adult children.

Reflection

Reflection

Reflection

Reflection